Everyday Chip Carving Designs

48 Stylish and Practical Projects

Wayne Barton

Marty Leenhouts

Barry McKenzie

Bruce Nicholas

Tatiana Baldina

FOX CHAPEL
PUBLISHING

A *Woodcarving Illustrated* Book
WoodcarvingIllustrated.com

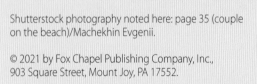

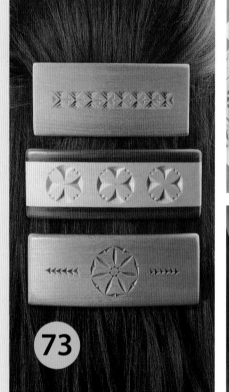

© 2021 by Fox Chapel Publishing Company, Inc., 903 Square Street, Mount Joy, PA 17552.

ISBN 978-1-4971-0171-5

Library of Congress Control Number: 2021936074.

To learn more about the other great books from Fox Chapel Publishing, or to find a retailer near you, call toll-free 800-457-9112 or visit us at *foxchapelpublishing.com*.

We are always looking for talented authors. To submit an idea, please send a brief inquiry to acquisitions@foxchapelpublishing.com.

Printed in China
First printing

41

Contents

Introduction

Chip carving as an art form has been around for thousands of years. The classic "chip carved" look—featuring precise groupings of geometric shapes set into a smooth surface—appears on grand cathedrals throughout Europe from the 12th century on. But the style has also adorned humbler, homier objects, from folk art toys to boxes and drinking vessels. These items were not simply decorative; they had an everyday function around the house. And they could be carved by newcomers to the craft, using just one or two simple tools.

In this spirit, we've gathered some of the best chip carving projects from our archive, including cereal bowls, barrettes, coffee spoons, holiday ornaments, and even a cribbage board. Each one is both elegant and practical—and many, such as Roman Chernikov's "Summery Supernova Coasters" (page 49), can be completed in an afternoon. If this is your first time picking up a knife, don't worry—we've included tips and techniques from today's leading chip carvers, such as Wayne Barton, Marty Leenhouts, and Charlene Lynum, to guide you through your first cuts.

Happy carving from the *Woodcarving Illustrated* team!

Hannah Carroll
Jon Deck
Kaylee Schofield
Kelly Umenhofer

GETTING STARTED

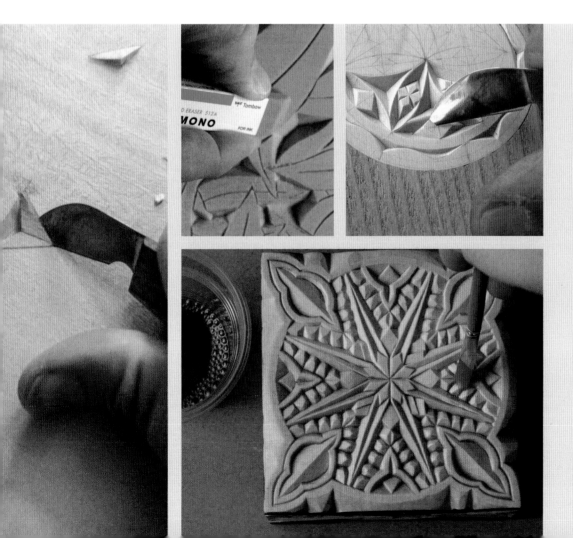

Materials & Tools

One of the wonderful things about chip carving is that you need a limited amount of materials and tools to begin—you may already have a few of the necessary items lying around your shop! The remainder can be found online or through craft or carving supply stores.

Knives

The two main knife varieties used for chip carving are the cutting knife and the stab knife.

The cutting knife is the primary knife used in chip carving. The carver typically holds the knife at a 65° angle for most actions. When kept very sharp, it can be used to cut two-corner, three-corner, four-corner, free-form, and even layered chips cleanly on a variety of flat or rounded surfaces.

The stab knife is used to incise decorative elements into the wood, embellishing an existing design. The carver typically holds the handle perpendicular to the surface of the blank, rocking the blade quickly along its sharp edge. Unlike the cutting knife, this tool is typically not used to remove chips of wood.

Wood

The two main types of wood used for chip carving are basswood (known as linden or limewood in countries outside the United States) and butternut.

Basswood is light-colored and soft with a consistent, tight grain. Beginning carvers often start with basswood, as it is well suited to a range of carving styles, including chip carving, caricature carving, and relief carving.

Butternut, part of the walnut family, is a medium-brown color and is slightly harder than basswood. However, its tight structure and striking grain make it an elegant choice for certain projects, particularly those where deeper cuts are required.

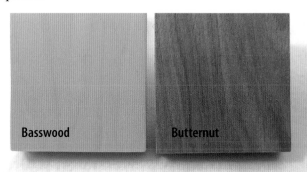

Basswood   Butternut

Additional Items

If you're building a chip carving kit for the first time, these items will also come in handy.

Bow compass – used to apply symmetrical designs to a piece of wood.

Graphite transfer paper – used to transfer a photocopied or sketched design onto the wood.

Mechanical pencil – used to sketch pattern elements and center points onto the wood, either directly or in combination with graphite transfer paper.

Sandpaper – occasionally used to remove lingering pattern lines or smooth certain areas on a carving. *Note: The beauty of chip carving lies in its crisp lines and stark geometry. It is not recommended to sand the entire surface of a project after carving.*

Sharpening tools – used to maintain chip carving knives so they cut cleanly without tearing the wood. A leather strop and honing compound or a set of ceramic sharpening stones works nicely.

T square or ruler – used for drawing straight lines on the surface of the blank.

White eraser – used to remove lingering pattern lines without smudging.

Pattern Transfer

Chip carving is a precise art, so finding a method of accurate pattern transfer that works for you is key. There are many ways to transfer a pattern to the wood blank before carving, but two of the most common are the following:

Graphite Paper

1. Place the pattern right side up on the center of the project. Secure one edge with tape, lift the pattern, and slide a piece of graphite paper between the pattern and the wood, dark side down.
2. Replace the pattern on top of the graphite paper and sketch along the pattern lines with a colored pencil. This way, you can see which lines you've already drawn.

Heat Transfer

1. Use a laser printer or copier to make a mirror-image printout of the pattern. Place it face down in the center of the project and secure one side with tape so it doesn't slide around.
2. Go over the surface of the paper with a heat transfer tool, never staying in one spot for too long. Check your work as you go to ensure the pattern transfer is successful.

1

Tape down one end of the pattern and slide the graphite paper under it, facedown.

1

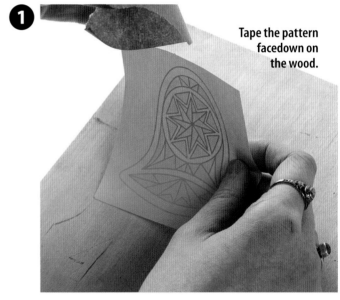

Tape the pattern facedown on the wood.

2

Follow the pattern lines with a colored pencil or pen.

2

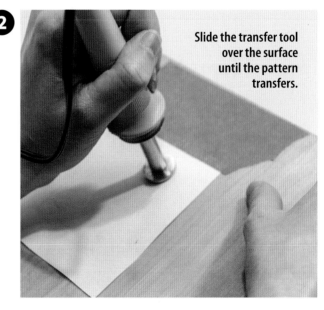

Slide the transfer tool over the surface until the pattern transfers.

Five Basic Chip Cuts

Most chip carving projects will include these five basic cuts. Practice each on scrap wood until you can produce them consistently.

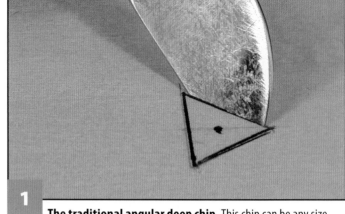

1 **The traditional angular deep chip.** This chip can be any size, as long as the cuts all converge at the deepest point in the middle of the chip. Hold the knife at the same angle to make all of the cuts. After you free the chip, go back and lightly carve into the corner to remove any splintered wood and clean up the chip.

2 **The shallow chip.** Draw the chip the same as the angular deep chip, but cut it differently. Make vertical cuts on both sides of the triangle. The deepest cuts are at the triangle's point and decrease in depth as you approach the triangle's base. Hold the knife nearly horizontal and cut from one side of the base to the other, sliding the tip of the knife up to the deepest part of the chip at the tip of the triangle.

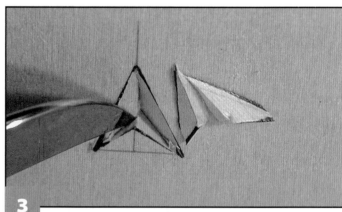

3 **The old-world-style chip.** Traditionally made using chisels, gouges, and skew knives, this chip can be made with a chip carving knife. It requires two angular cuts and two vertical cuts. Hold the knife at an angle and cut along the two sides of the large triangle towards the point of the small triangle. Make two vertical cuts along the sides of the small triangle to release the chip. Do not remove the wood for the small triangle.

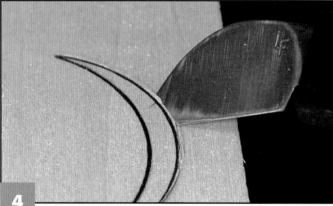

4 **The flare or free-form angular line cut.** Establish the bottom of the chip with the first cut, and free the chip with the second cut. The angle at which you hold the blade changes depending on the depth and width of the line. As the chip gets deeper, the angle increases until the knife is nearly vertical. For the shallow areas, the angle decreases until the knife is nearly horizontal.

5 **The straight line cut.** Establish the bottom of the chip with the first cut and release the chip with the second cut. Depending on the width of the line, you may need to make short cuts on either end of the line to free the chip. The blade is held at an identical angle while making all of the cuts. The depth of the cut is the same from end to end.

Applying Finishes

This step is crucial to the presentation of your art; a poorly executed finish can detract from the beauty of the carving, rather than enhance it. Here are a few common finishing methods to try:

Clear Finish

Simple and understated, this method puts the shadows in your carved piece on full display. Just apply two to four coats of brush-on or spray-on polyurethane to the surface of the carved piece, letting dry and sanding very lightly between coats. You could also use a clear lacquer. This method is preferred by regular *Woodcarving Illustrated* contributors Charlene Lynum and Marty Leenhouts.

Gel Stain

Bold and dramatic, this method adds contrast to your carved piece by making use of differences in grain absorption. The cut areas will absorb finish at a higher rate than the uncarved areas, making for shadowy chips set into a lighter surface. First, seal the carving with clear polyurethane, allowing time for the wood to absorb the sealer. Then wipe off the excess with a rag. Once dry, apply your preferred gel stain over the surface with a paintbrush. Wipe off the stain right away, making sure to remove any globs from the crannies. When dry, spray with more clear polyurethane. This method is preferred by master carver Wayne Barton.

Clear finish.

Gel stain.

Alternate Method: Finishing Before You Start

This method produces a dramatic effect distinct from the gel stain technique. Before carving, seal the blank with polyurethane and let dry. Then apply gel stain to the entire surface and let dry completely. Apply the pattern using your preferred method, and then carve through the stain in the specified areas. Once all of the chips are carved, finish with a clear coat of your choice.

Setting Up Your Workspace

Take the time to properly prepare your workspace so that your chip carving experience is safe and enjoyable. Work in a well-ventilated space and surround your carving setup with good, even lighting. Daylight-rated bulbs are a great option. Place an old sheet of plywood under your workpiece or use a Carver's Lapboard (page 11) to catch the chips.

Practice Boards

One of the main challenges for beginners is knowing how deeply to undercut a facet or how much pressure to apply with a knife. Practice boards are great tools for building muscle memory around these techniques. Use a premade board or create your own. Transfer the pattern using your preferred method (page 7). Be sure to leave enough blank space to experiment and practice the five basic cuts (page 8).

Safety

Although chip carvers produce more chips than dust, preparing blanks makes enough dust to be a potential concern. When using power tools such as drum sanders and band saws, employ a benchtop dust collector to protect your lungs and help keep your work area clean. Wear a dust mask and safety googles, tie up long hair, and secure loose clothing. Before you sit down to carve, invest in a carving glove and thumb guard, and stretch your wrists and fingers periodically to ensure that you can chip carve without difficulty for years to come.

Practice boards are great tools to learn basic chip carving skills needed for more challenging projects.

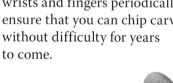

Use carving gloves and a thumb guard to protect your hands from errant cuts.

Construct a shop-made dust collector by encasing a standard box fan in a wooden frame with furnace filters. Sandwich the fan between the filters, using a lower-efficiency filter on the intake side and a high-efficiency HEPA filter on the exhaust side.

Making a Carver's Lapboard

By Gary MacKay

W hen I first started chip carving, I would place a towel on my lap to catch the chips. With chip carving, you should have your thumb, knuckle, and knife point in contact with the wood you are carving. That's not normally possible when you carve the chips near the edge of the blank. To help support my hand while I carve these chips, I created a lapboard.

I made my lapboard with 1½" (3.8cm)-wide sides to allow plenty of surface contact when carving chips near the edges of my stock. The sides are the same thickness as the wood I normally carve and help to lock the blank in place. Additionally, the lapboard gives me a solid surface to carve on and I can sweep the chips into the drilled recesses to keep them out of the way while I work.

If you increase the height of the sides, you can use the lapboard to hold extra tools and catch wood chips when you work on any type of carving.

materials & tools

MATERIALS
- Plywood, ¾" (1.9cm) thick: base, 10" x 12" (25.4cm x 30.5cm)
- Scrap wood, ⅜" (1cm) thick: long side, 1½" x 12" (3.8cm x 30.5cm)
- Scrap wood ⅜" (1cm) thick: short side, 1½" x 7" (3.8cm x 17.8cm)
- Wood glue

TOOLS
- Drill press with bit: 1½" (38mm)- to 2" (51mm)-dia. Forstner
- Clamps
- Chip carving knife

The author used these products for the project. Substitute your choice of brands, tools, and materials as desired.

Step 1: Cut the sides to size. I chip carve mainly ⅜" (1cm)-thick wood, so my sides are ⅜" (1cm) thick by 1½" (3.8cm) wide. The length of the sides depends on the size of the lapboard you want to make.

Step 2: Cut the base to size. I made my lapboard 10" by 12" (25.4cm by 30.5cm), but you can size the board according to the scrap wood you have or what is most convenient for you.

Step 3: Drill the chip collection holes.
Use the drawing to determine the position of the holes. I use a 1½" (38mm)-diameter Forstner bit to drill ¼" (6mm)-deep holes. *Note: Alternatively, cut a piece of ¼" (6mm)-thick plywood to the size of the base and drill the holes with a spade bit. Glue the ¼" (6mm)-thick plywood to a ½" (1.3cm)-thick piece to get the ¾" (1.9cm)-thick base.*

Step 4: Assemble the lapboard. Glue and clamp the sides to the base.

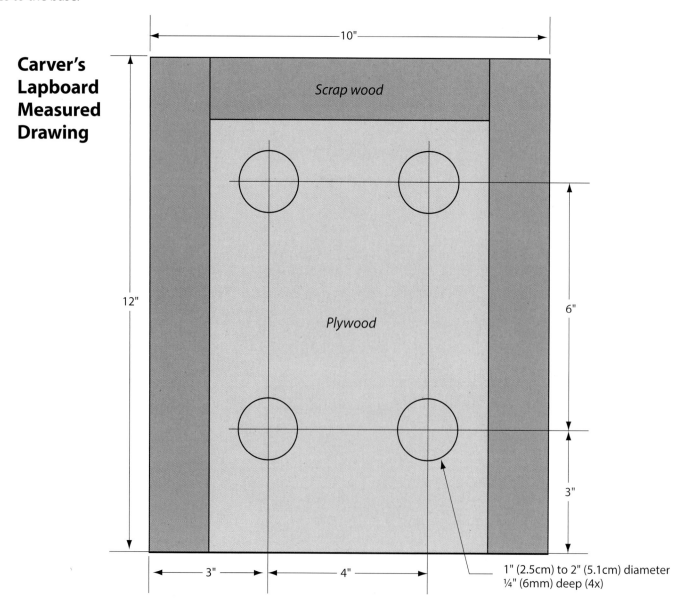

Carver's Lapboard Measured Drawing

10"

Scrap wood

12"

Plywood

6"

3"

3"

4"

1" (2.5cm) to 2" (5.1cm) diameter ¼" (6mm) deep (4x)

Simple Coaster

By Marty Leenhouts

Carving this swirl rosette without a center chip missing is a challenge most carvers will enjoy. But don't expect perfection the first time. Learn as you go and self-evaluate along the way. And make sure your knife is scary sharp!

Getting Started

Pre-sand the blank to 320-grit until no marks remain. Apply the pattern using either a photocopy and a Pattern Transfer Tool or graphite transfer paper and a pencil.

materials & tools

MATERIALS
- Basswood, ½" (1.3cm) thick: 4" (10.2cm) square
- Self-adhesive cork backing: 4" (10.2cm) square
- Sandpaper: assorted grits up to 320
- Pencil
- Graphite transfer paper (optional)
- Gel stain, such as Varathane® Ipswitch pine
- Clear finish, such as spray matte acrylic or satin lacquer
- Tombow Sand Eraser

TOOLS
- Chip carving knife
- Foam brush (for applying stain)
- Pattern Transfer Tool
- Vacuum

The author used these products for the project. Substitute your choice of brands, tools, and materials as desired.

Carving and Finishing

Carve the piece. Grain direction is important when it comes to determining where to make your first cut. Make sure your first cut goes with the grain from the outside to the inside. When your cut reaches the delicate center region where all of the chips meet, lighten the grip on your knife and gently drag the knife to the center. A light grip will equal a light cut.

Continue making these same outside-in cuts on just the left side of each three-corner chip, moving around the swirl in a counterclockwise direction. When you're back at the beginning, start the second round of cuts, this time on just the right side of each three-corner chip. Start each of these cuts from the inside out where your very last outside-in cut ended. Keep a light grip on your knife, increasing the depth on your cut as you reach the outside of the swirl. Make the third cut to remove the chip. Then rotate your work in a clockwise direction so that each second cut can be made along the edge of the chip just removed. This will create a nice, sharp ridge between chips. Then remove the small outside chips.

Remove any leftover pattern lines with a Tombow Sand Eraser. Apply a finish. I sprayed on four coats of clear matte acrylic. Lightly sand and vacuum off any dust before adding the final coat.

Simple Coaster Pattern

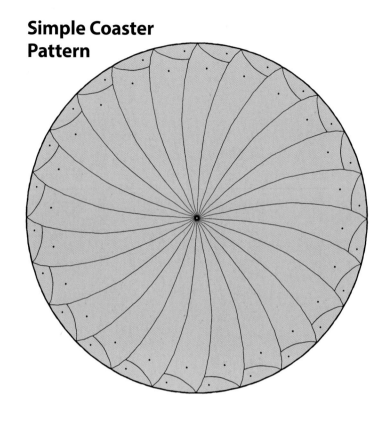

Cut Direction Diagram

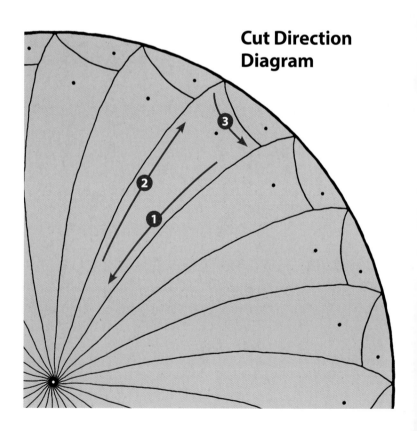

PROJECTS FOR HOSTING

Pineapple Welcome Sign

By Vernon DePauw

The pineapple has long been a symbol of welcome and hospitality. Rather than carving down the entire surface of the sign, we'll carve and attach the pineapple separately. Then we'll use a simple system to carve the letters and learn how to add a glow with gold leaf.

Getting Started

Enlarge the patterns as desired, and then transfer the outlines to the blanks. Cut the perimeter of the sign and the pineapple.

CARVING THE PINEAPPLE

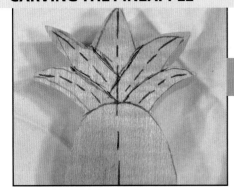

1 **Mark the center of the pineapple fruit and leaves.** These lines will be the highest (thickest) part of the fruit and each leaf.

2 **Carve the leaves.** Use a carving knife. Leave the centers thick, and carve a groove between the leaves.

3 **Round the fruit from the centerline to the edges.** Use the knife.

4 **Undercut the back edge of the pineapple the entire way around.** Add the details to the fruit and leaves.

CARVING THE LETTERS

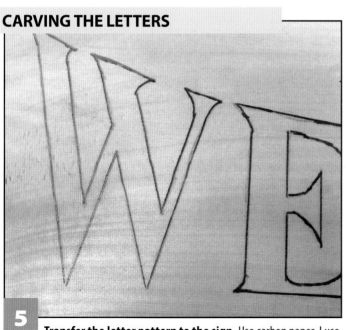

5

Transfer the letter pattern to the sign. Use carbon paper. I use Times New Roman font, which is a serif font. Serifs are the decorative elements added to the basic form of each letter, and I like the look of serif fonts for carving.

materials & **tools**

MATERIALS

- Basswood, ¾" (1.9cm) thick: sign, 8" x 20" (20.3cm x 50.8cm); pineapple, 3" x 4" (7.6cm x 10.2cm)
- Carbon paper
- Pencil
- Drywall screws, #8: 2 each, 1⅝" (4.1cm) long
- Latex house primer: light gray
- Latex house paint: white
- Milk paint, such as Olde Century®: goldenrod yellow (optional), hemlock green (optional), settlers blue
- Baby powder
- Gold leaf, 23-karat loose: at least 5 leaves
- Gilding size: slow set, such as Rolco clear oil
- Wood glue
- Spar urethane, such as Helmsman®: clear satin
- Sandpaper: 220-grit

TOOLS

- Band saw
- Drill with bit: ⁵⁄₃₂" (4mm)-dia.
- Chip carving knife
- Screwdriver
- Paintbrushes: ¼" (6mm)-wide angled shader, ½" (13mm)-wide angled shader, 1" (25mm)-wide artist, ½" (13mm)-wide soft craft, 1" (25mm)-wide soft craft
- Small sponge

The author used these products for the project. Substitute your choice of brands, tools, and materials as desired.

6 **Carve the serifs.** Use the knife to make a three-sided chip-style cut for each of the serifs.

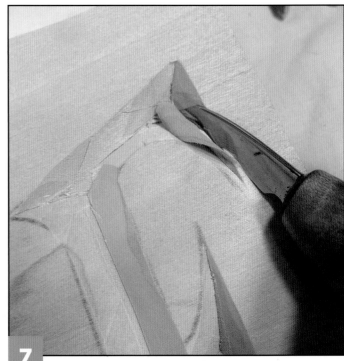

7 **Make angled cuts along the inside and outside of each letter.** Use the carving knife. Make the cuts meet in the center to create a V-shaped groove. Refine the edges of the letters. Use the knife. Create crisp edges to give the letters depth and sharpness.

FINISHING THE PROJECT

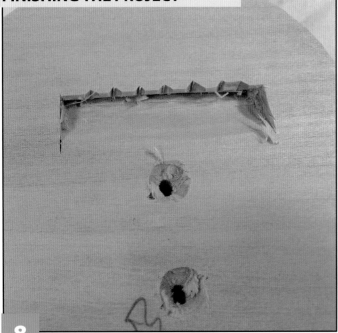

8 **Carve the outside edge of the sign.** You could also soften the edges with 220-grit sandpaper. Position the pineapple and trace around it. Drill two ⁵⁄₃₂" (4mm)-dia. holes through the sign inside the outline and countersink these holes from the back with the screws used to attach the pineapple to the sign. Carve a hanging slot in the center of the sign back. Sand the top surface of the sign to remove any reference lines and prepare it for painting. Apply a little wood glue to the back of the pineapple and hold it in position while driving a screw in from the back. Rotate the pineapple so it is straight up and down, and secure it with the second screw.

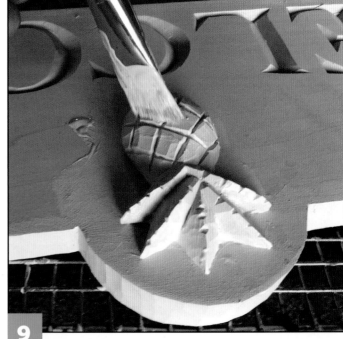

9 **Apply two light coats of light gray exterior house primer on all sides of the sign.** I use a light gray because it is easier to cover with a topcoat than white. Use a 1" (25mm)-wide artist brush to spread the paint evenly into the grooves and letters you have carved. Make sure the light coats do not fill in the carved details.

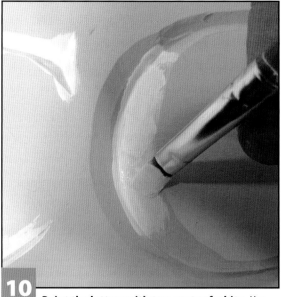

10   **Paint the letters with two coats of white.** Use a ¼" (6mm)-wide angled shader. Do the letters first because you can paint up to their edges when painting the top surface to produce crisp lines. Paint the pineapple fruit goldenrod yellow and the leaves hemlock green, or, if you plan to gild it with gold leaf (see Applying Gold Leaf, page 20), apply two coats of settlers blue to the pineapple and the sign surface front and back. Apply two coats of Helmsman clear satin spar urethane, front and back.

page 20

TIP

PICKING PAINT COLORS

When picking sign colors, keep in mind that you want to create a contrast between the sign, the pineapple, and the letters. To give my sign a Colonial look, I used Olde Century Colors simulated milk paint, which comes in traditional colors and leaves a subtle brush strokes in the finish, like paint from the 1800s.

Welcome Sign Pattern

Each block of this grid equals 1" in proportion to the original pattern. Enlarge this art to 200%, or to desired size.

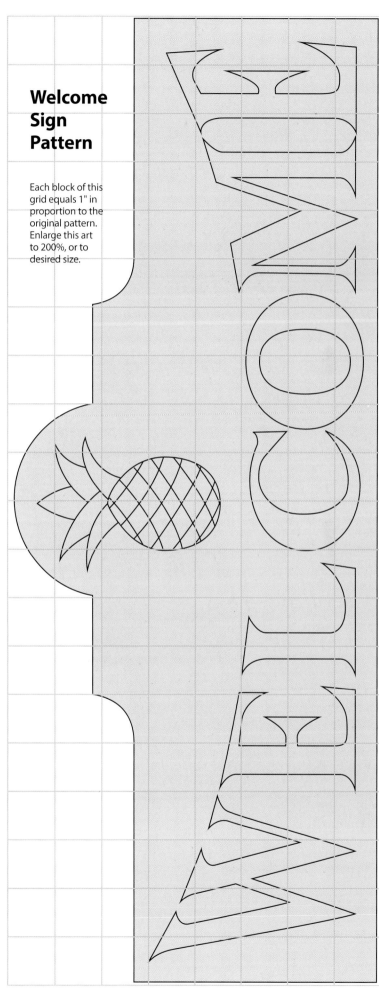

Applying Gold Leaf

Choosing Materials

The best gold leaf to use for a carving project is 23-karat genuine gold leaf in loose leaf form. It comes in "books," usually of 25 gold sheets, but some suppliers sell five or ten leaf booklets. For one pineapple, five leaves of gold should be more than enough. Avoid imitation gold, which lacks the luster of real gold and is difficult to apply to a wood carving.

The glue used to attach gold leaf to the carving is called "gilding size." It comes in two drying speeds: slow set and quick set. I prefer slow set because it has a longer open time, which gives you plenty of time to apply the gold. I use soft ½" (13mm)- and 1" (25mm)-wide soft bristle craft brushes to apply the gold leaf and move it into the grooves and crevices.

Getting Started

Gold leaf will stick to any surface with even the slightest stickiness to it. To reduce the amount of gold that may stick where you do not want it, first let the sign dry for a few weeks. Use a damp cloth to wipe down the entire sign to remove any remaining stickiness. Then, wipe it dry and let it air-dry overnight. Lightly sprinkle a layer of baby powder over the sign, blowing off any extra. Prepare your work area by turning off any fans or vents, because air movement will affect the even drying of the sizing as well as the application of the gold.

Applying Gold Leaf

A. Apply the sizing evenly. Use a ½" (13mm)-wide angled shader brush. Apply an even coat to the surfaces and grooves you want gold to stick to, but do not allow it to puddle or run. Thick areas of sizing will dry at a different rate than thin areas.

B. Check the tack of the sized surface. The sizing will dry at different rates based on the humidity and the thickness of the application. Gilding on wet sizing will use a lot of gold and dull the luster. To avoid those problems, let the size dry for six to eight hours, and then check the tack. I use the hairs on the back of my finger. Turn your hand over and slowly lower it to just above the surface until the sizing tugs on the hairs between your knuckles. A gentle tug, like when a mosquito brushes your hair, indicates the size is ready. A tug strong enough to actually pull your hair indicates the size is too wet. As a second test, place a small piece of gold on the sized area, and then see if another small piece will stick to the gold you just placed. If the second piece sticks, the sizing is too wet. Wet sizing will pass through the thin gold leaf and allow the next piece to stick on top. Check the size often until the tack is ready.

C. Fold back one page of the gold leaf book to expose the gold. Swish the 1" (25mm)-wide brush through your hair to add a little static and oil to the brush. Lower the brush to the leaf; the static will cause a small piece to lift to the brush. Move the gold slowly to the pineapple surface and gently lower it until it sticks to the surface. Continue transferring gold from the book to the carving until the pineapple is covered.

D. Gently brush the pineapple to set the gold in place. Use the 1" (25mm)-wide brush. This should make most of the gold stick to the surface, although some small pieces will flake off. Brush the small pieces into the grooves, adding more gold from the book as needed to cover all of the surfaces and grooves. Brush over the entire pineapple to dislodge any loose gold. If gold will not stick in an area, brush a thin coat of sizing on it, let the sizing set to the proper tack, and reapply the gold.

E. Wipe the gilded area with a clean, damp sponge. This gives it a clean, finished look. Don't add a topcoat over the gold; it may dull the fine luster. If a piece of gold sticks in the wrong place, gently scrape it off with the back of a carving knife.

Cozy
Candle Plate

By Wayne Barton

While the design possibilities for chip carving are endless and have been executed for centuries with a broad array of tools, truly pleasing work can be done relatively quickly with only one or two knives. Since the surface to be carved is already established, laying out the pattern is simple. While it is not necessary to draw a line in the layout for every cut to be made, the more definition given to the layout, the less you will need to guess exactly where to cut. For me, creating the design is often half the fun.

materials & **tools**

MATERIALS
- Basswood plate, 10" (25.4cm)-dia., with outside bead on rim and 3" (7.6cm) x ¼" (6mm)-deep well in center
- Mechanical pencil with B-grade lead
- Finish: satin polyurethane spray
- Gel stain: brown mahogany
- Sandpaper: 220-grit

TOOLS
- Compass
- Ruler
- Eraser
- Knives: chip carving, stab
- Stiff bristle brush

The author used these products for the project. Substitute your choice of brands, tools, and materials as desired.

1   **Determine the center of the plate.** Draw two perpendicular lines across the center of the plate. The lines cross at the center. Use the center point to draw in all of the circles needed to lay out the design. Running from the first drawn circle to the edge of the plate on both sides, draw a straight line through the center of the plate parallel to the grain of the wood. Bisect this line and establish a vertical line.

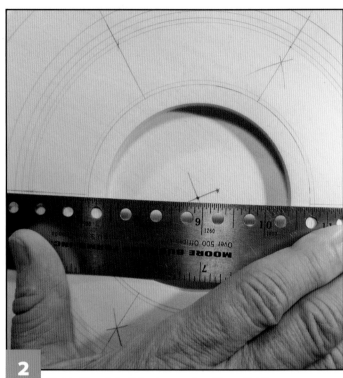

2   **Divide the plate into six equal sections.** Set the compass to the same radius as the first drawn circle. Place the point of the compass where the vertical line intersects the first circle and make a mark on the circle both to the left and the right. Repeat the procedure at the other intersection of the vertical line and the first circle. Use a ruler to draw lines through the marks, creating six sections.

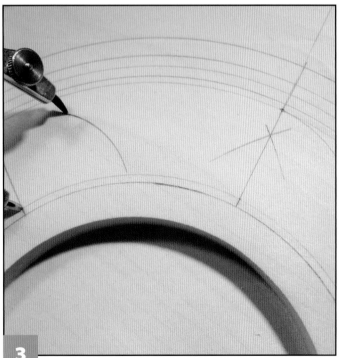

3   **Space out the fans.** The fans are located between the second and third circles. Place the point of the compass on the intersection of the second circle and the line defining one of the six sections. Set the compass so it reaches the third drawn circle. Draw an arch from the second circle to the point where the third circle intersects with the line. Repeat for each of the six sections.

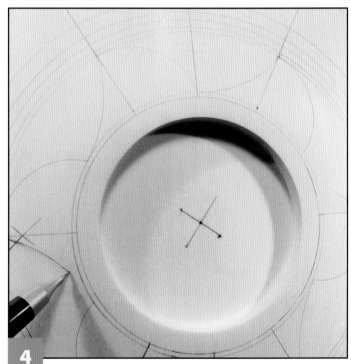

4   **Outline the fans.** Draw a smoothly curved freehand line connecting the top of one arch to the bottom of the adjacent arch. Repeat to complete the outline for all twelve fans.

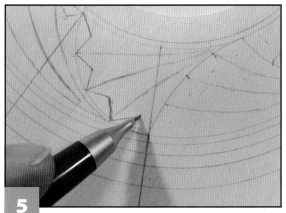

5 **Finish drawing the fan motif.** Divide each fan into four equal sections. Draw a triangle at the large end of each section. There is a narrow ring around both edges of the fan motif.

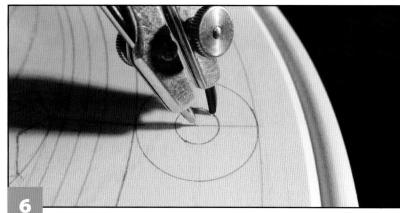

6 **Space out the flowers.** The foliage motif is located within the last two circles. Draw circles centered on each of the lines defining the six sections. The diameter of the circle is equal to the width of the section. Draw a ¼" (6mm)-diameter circle centered inside each of these circles. These circles will become the centers of the five-petaled flowers.

7 **Draw in the foliated pattern.** Find the center between each of the two circles and draw a ¼" (6mm)-high diamond touching the inside circle. Set the compass to draw an arch from the top of the diamond to the bottom of the circle. Make the arch from the bottom of one circle to the bottom of the next circle in one pass. Use this arch as a guide to draw or trace the leaf design between the circles.

8 **Draw in the three-cornered chips.** We are left with four rings between the fan motif and the foliated motif. The first ring outside the fan motif will be carved. The three-cornered chips will be located on the center of the remaining three rings. Space out the chips by dividing each of the sections in half and then in half again until you have sixteen sections. I use dots to define the chips.

CARVING THE CHIPS

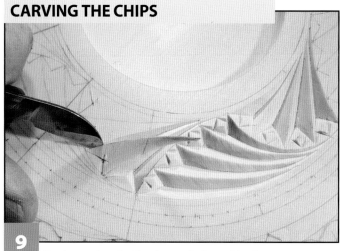

9 **Begin carving the fan.** I carve the large chips first to prevent the wood from breaking out later. Make the first cuts to define the triangles at the top of each of the four fan sections. Then carve the long chips up to these cuts to shape the fans. The tips of the fans, opposite of the triangles, are staggered and do not come together at a single point.

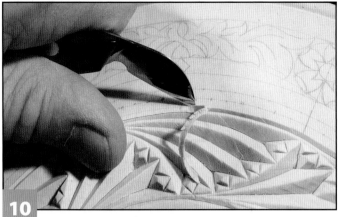

10 **Finish carving the fan.** Carve the small notches in the triangles at the ends of the fans. Then carve the two narrow rings on either side of the fans. Make the first cut on both rings, angling away from the fans to prevent breakout. Then carve the second side of the rings.

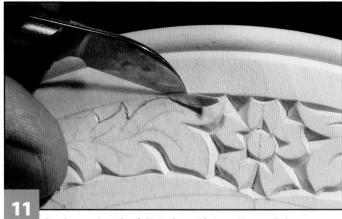

11 **Begin carving the foliated motif.** Carve the small chips that define the leaves and flowers. Make the cuts bordering the leaves or flowers first, then make the cut around the border to free the chips. Use a stab knife to accent the petals.

12 **Carve the large chips under the leaves.** Make the cuts around the diamond shape first. Then make the long angled cuts up to the diamond. Cut next to the foliage first, and then cut along the border to free the chip. This sequence of cuts minimizes breakout.

13 **Carve the small chips.** Use the dot on the line closest to the foliage as the point of the triangle. Carve the three-corner chips, maintaining the same angle on the cuts so the deepest part of the cut is in the center. Then cut small, shallow three-corner chips in the remaining triangles.

Staining and Finishing

Erase all of the remaining pencil lines. Use an ink eraser to remove stubborn pencil lines. Be careful not to flatten the sharp ridges of the fan motif.

Experiment with the finishing technique on a sample piece of the same type of wood. Apply a thin coat of sealer, such as spray polyurethane, to the carving. This allows the wood to accept the stain evenly and prevents blotching. Sand the finish lightly with 220-grit sandpaper to remove any raised grain. Apply a coat of brown mahogany gel stain with a stiff bristle brush. Work the gel into all of the carved recesses. Start with the back of the plate and then move to the front. Immediately wipe off the excess stain and use a brush to remove the excess stain from the carved recesses. Allow the stain to dry and apply a second coat of stain, if desired. After the stain is fully dry, apply two or three light coats of satin polyurethane, sanding lightly between coats. Do not sand after the final coat. Add a candle to the center.

Cozy Candle Plate Patterns

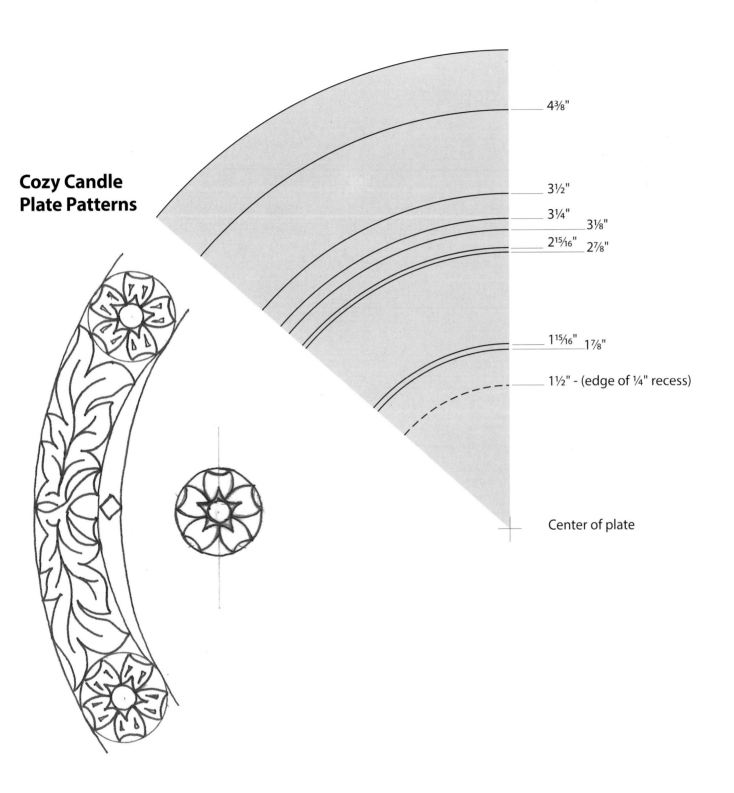

4⅜"

3½"

3¼"

3⅛"

2¹⁵⁄₁₆" 2⅞"

1¹⁵⁄₁₆" 1⅞"

1½" - (edge of ¼" recess)

Center of plate

Modern Chess Set

By Barry McKenzie

Chess was invented in India around the 6th century A.D. This set combines one of the oldest forms of carving with one of the oldest board games. Although the set is highly decorative and makes a beautiful display, it is fully functional and quite durable.

I use standard design elements to distinguish the pieces. The king has a cross on top, connecting it with the Crusades. The queen has a crown identifying her royalty. The knight is a stylized representation of a knight's horse. The bishop has a top much like a Pope's miter. The rook's top represents the ramparts of a medieval castle wall.

The set looks challenging, but in reality, you only need to master five basic cuts to complete it. The trick is reproducing these cuts consistently. I used simple chips to embellish the game board, but it could be left as a solid surface. The design for the board squares is rotated and repeated to create the overall pattern.

I used basswood and butternut for my set. Both woods are well suited for chip carving. You could also carve the entire set from basswood and use stains to distinguish the opposing sides.

materials & tools

MATERIALS

- Basswood, 1⅜" (3.5cm) square: light pieces, 34" (86.4cm) long
- Butternut, 1⅜" (3.5cm) square: dark pieces, 34" (86.4cm) long
- Basswood, 1" (2.5cm) thick: light squares, 5 each 1¾" x 9½" (4.4cm x 24.1cm)
- Butternut, 1" (2.5cm) thick: dark squares, 4 each 1¾" x 9½" (4.4cm x 24.1cm)
- Sandpaper: assorted grits to 220
- Clear finish, such as low gloss or satin
- Polyurethane finish
- Gel stain, such as Varathane® Ipswitch pine (optional)
- Clean rags
- Craft felt: dark green
- Cyanoacrylate (CA) glue
- Graphite transfer paper (optional)
- Mechanical pencil
- Wood molding (for game board) (optional)

TOOLS

- Chip carving knife
- Saw of choice
- Disc sander or belt sander
- Paintbrushes: assorted
- Ruler
- Stylus (optional)
- Clamps (optional)

The author used these products for the project. Substitute your choice of brands, tools, and materials as desired.

Finishing

The process detailed below will keep the chips looking crisp and clean-cut, and prevent the finish from seeping out of the edges of the chip cavity.

Step 1: Seal the main surface. Brush a light amount of finish on the exterior surface, avoiding the chip cavities. Use a ½" (13mm)-wide, stiff artists' brush. Tilt the wood to reflect light off the surface and spot any areas missing finish or stain.

Step 2: Seal the edges of the chips. Brush additional finish on the surface, getting some finish around the top edge of the chip cavities, but not inside the cavities. Swipe a damp brush across the top of the chips.

Step 3: Add finish to the chip cavities. Wet the surface much more than the first two applications, and get some finish down inside the top edge of the cavities. Do not flood the cavity. Swipe a wet brush across the top and slightly over the edge of the cavity.

Step 4: Flood the chip cavity. Fill the cavities with finish. Before the finish starts to dry, wipe off the surface, the top of the chips, and down in the cavities with a soft rag. Continue brushing with a dry brush to remove the excess finish.

Step 5: Accent the chip cavities. Flood the chip cavities with light-colored stain, and immediately remove as much finish as possible with a rag. Then brush with a dry brush until you remove all of the finish from the cavities. *Note: This step is optional.*

Step 6: Apply a second coat of finish. If the chip cavities look dull, flood the cavities with more finish. Remove as much finish as possible with a rag, and brush the chips with a dry brush to remove all of the finish from the cavities. You can apply an additional coat to give the project a high gloss finish. Use cyanoacrylate (CA) glue to attach a small square of green felt to the bottom of each chess piece.

Practice different cuts on each piece and build a game board fit for royalty.

The Game Board

Cut nine 1" by 1 ¾" by 9½" (2.5cm by 4.4cm by 2.4cm) strips, five of basswood and four of butternut. Glue them together in an alternating pattern. After the glue has dried, cut the blank into eight 1 ¾" (4.4cm)-wide strips (the extra length offsets the wood removed by the saw with each cut). Offset the strips by one entire square to produce the alternating dark and light pattern. Glue the strips in place, and then cut off the overhanging squares.

Carving the Game Board

All of the squares use the same pattern, but the image used to embellish the dark squares is rotated 90° to create an overall pattern for the entire board. Use a shallow chip technique to remove the light areas of the pattern. You can also embellish the chips with a thin, shallow line cut at the base of the triangles. To complete the game board and give it a polished look, miter-cut commercial molding and edge glue it around the squares to serve as a frame.

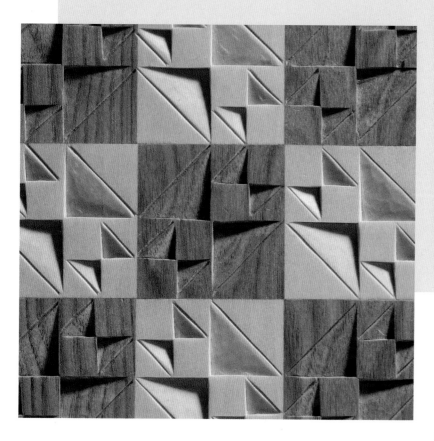

Modern Chess Set Game Board Pattern

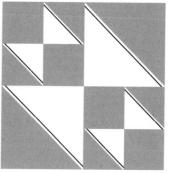

This pattern is used for both white and dark squares.

King

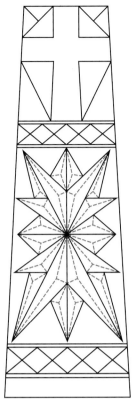

Modern Chess Set Patterns

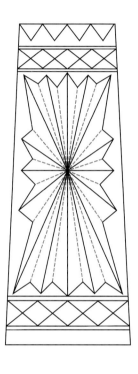

Queen

Knight

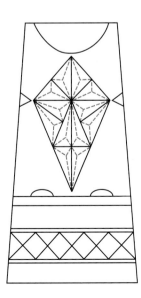

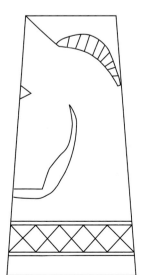

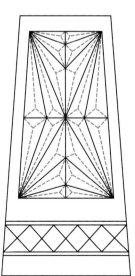

Modern Chess Set Patterns

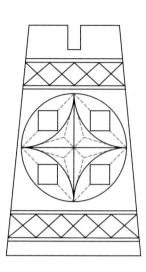

Rook

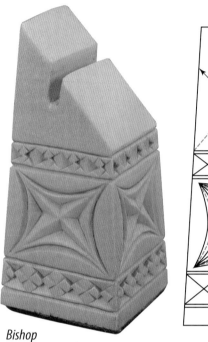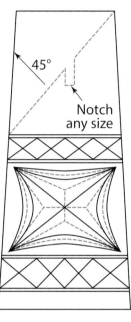

45°

Notch any size

Bishop

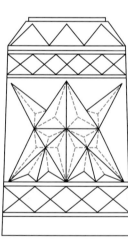

Pawn

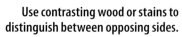

Use contrasting wood or stains to distinguish between opposing sides.

Art Deco Light Switch Cover

By Ben Mayfield

These days, home owners are leaning toward a more customized look for their homes. Light switch covers are a quick and easy way to add unique handcarved accents to home décor.

My first light switch covers included screw holes to secure them in place. While fitting the covers, I realized that if the center hole was cut to fit tightly around the switch, screws were unnecessary.

I've provided a pattern to get you started, but I encourage you to be creative and design your own patterns. Enlarge the opening and use the panel to embellish a doorbell or carve two panels and make a custom napkin holder.

materials & tools

MATERIALS

- Basswood, 5⁄16" (8mm) thick: 3¼" x 5½" (8.3cm x 14cm)
- Sandpaper: assorted grits
- Oil-based stain or tung oil
- Pre-stain wood conditioner (if using stain)
- Clear polyurethane
- Clean cloth

The author used these products for the project. Substitute your choice of brands, tools, and materials as desired.

TOOLS

- Scroll saw or coping saw
- Knives: detail, skew, chip carving
- #3 gouge: ⅛" (3mm), ⅝" (16mm)
- #5 gouges: ¼" (6mm), 9⁄16" (14mm)
- #6 gouge: 5⁄16" (8mm)
- V-tools: ¼" (6mm) 45°, ¼" (6mm) 70°
- Drill with bit: 1⁄16" (2mm)-dia.
- Compass
- Can of compressed air

MAKING THE CHIP CUTS

1 **Cut the blank.** Sand the surface smooth and transfer the pattern to the blank. Cut outside the perimeter of the pattern with a scroll saw and sand up to the line. I used a 150-grit sanding drum in a drill press. You can also use a belt sander or sand it by hand.

2 **Cut the triangular chips.** Angle the chip carving knife as you cut along the long lines of the triangles. Use light pressure at the point and increase the pressure as you approach the base to deepen the cut. The cuts should converge in the center. Make a deep cut along the base of the triangle to free the chip.

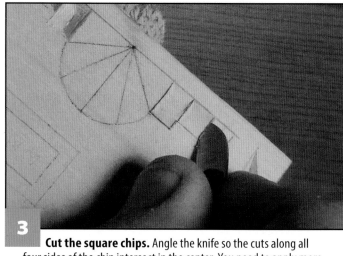

3 **Cut the square chips.** Angle the knife so the cuts along all four sides of the chip intersect in the center. You need to apply more pressure to make these cuts deeper than the cuts made in Step 2. Do not pry the chips out; deepen the cuts if necessary.

4 **Cut the rounded chips.** Carve along the two long sides using the technique explained in Step 2. Lightly score along the arc and gradually increase the depth of the cut until you free the chip. Clean up the cuts with a detail knife.

CARVING THE FAN

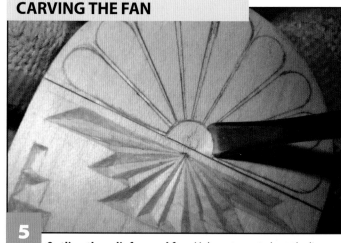

5 **Outline the relief carved fan.** Make a stop cut along the line that separates the fan from the chip carved section. Score the lines between the rays of the fan. Use a ¼" (6mm) #5 gouge to make deep stop cuts around the ends of the rays and the semicircle.

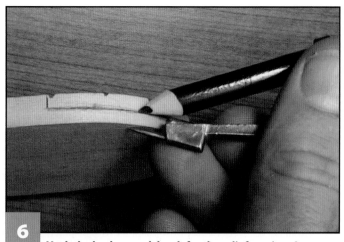

6 **Mark the background depth for the relief carving.** Set a compass to mark a line ⅛" (3mm) from the top of the blank. Trace this line along the edge of the blank. This line represents the depth of the background. Make a stop cut along the line with a knife.

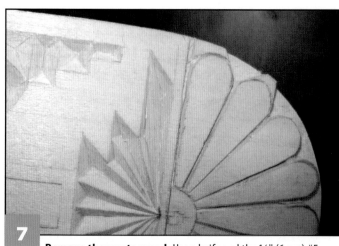

7 **Remove the waste wood.** Use a knife and the ¼" (6mm) #5 gouge. Remove all of the wood around the relief carved fan down to the background depth. Clean up the intersection between the fan and the background.

8 **Taper the fan rays.** Use a ⅝" (16mm) #3 gouge to taper the rays down, removing about 1⁄16" (2mm) from the end closest to the center semicircle. Do not cut into the semicircle. Deepen the cuts between the rays with a ¼" (6mm) 45° V-tool.

9 **Round the fan rays.** Use a detail knife or skew knife. Carefully remove the sharp corners to give the rays a soft rounded look. Deepen the cuts between the rays with a ¼" (6mm) 70° V-tool.

10 **Finish carving the fan.** Flip the ¼" (6mm) #5 gouge upside down to round the ends of the rays near the semicircle. Use a 9⁄16" (14mm) #5 gouge to shape the outside ends of the rays. Round the semicircle with the skew knife.

11 **Sand the fan.** I attach self-adhesive sandpaper to shop-made sanding tools to get into tight areas. Start with 120-grit and progress through the grits to 220.

PREPARING FOR INSTALLATION

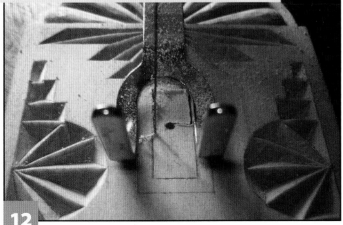

12 **Cut the switch hole.** Drill a blade-entry hole and cut the rectangle with a scroll saw or coping saw. Cut inside the line and sand the hole to fit the light switch. A tight fit eliminates the need to secure the plate with screws.

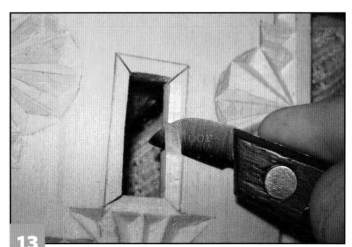

13 **Chamfer around the switch hole.** Make four deep stop cuts in the corners as indicated on the pattern. Lightly score the outside line around the switch hole. Make a cut at a 45° angle along all four sides of the switch hole.

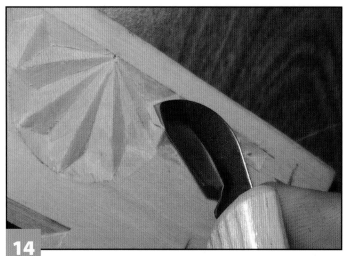

14 **Clean up the cuts.** Sharpen and strop your knife. Shave away any extra cut marks and clean up the corners. The goal is to make it look like the chips were removed with one cut per side.

15 **Hollow out the back of the carving.** Starting ⅛" (3mm) up from the bottom, draw a 1½" (3.8cm)-wide by 4⅛" (10.5cm)-long rectangle centered on the switch hole. Carve a ⅛" (3mm)-deep groove around the perimeter with the ¼" (6mm) 70° V-tool. Recess the rectangle with the gouges of your choice. Test the fit of the cover on your light switch. Make adjustments as needed.

Finishing the Cover

Sand the chip carved portion with 220-grit sandpaper to remove any pencil marks. Do not sand off the sharp edges of the chips. Remove the dust with compressed air. Sand it again with 320-grit sandpaper and remove the dust. Apply an oil finish or your finish of choice. If you plan to stain the cover, apply a little pre-stain wood conditioner to the flat surface. Do not allow the conditioner to seep into the cuts. The conditioner prevents the surface from absorbing as much stain as the cuts. While the conditioner is still wet, flood the carving with stain and allow it to set for five minutes. Wipe off the excess with a clean cloth. After the stain dries, you can add more stain for a darker look. Apply polyurethane to the completed project.

Art Deco Light Switch Cover Pattern

Family Photo Frame

By Marty Leenhouts

materials & **tools**

MATERIALS

- Picture frame, basswood: 7½" x 9½" (19.1cm x 24.1cm) or size of choice
- Graphite transfer paper
- Sandpaper: 220-grit or finer
- Tombow Sand Eraser
- Lacquer: spray satin
- Gel stain (optional)

TOOLS

- Chip carving knife, such as a diamond modified knife
- Pattern Transfer Tool (optional)
- Lazy Susan (optional)
- Nonslip mat (optional)

The author used these products for the project. Substitute your choice of brands, tools, and materials as desired.

The next time you need a unique frame for a print, diploma, or photograph, chip carve it yourself to make it extra special. Chip carving is easy to learn, and you can complete most projects with one knife.

Whether this frame will hang on your wall or be given away as a gift, knowing that you handcarved it will make the item inside even more meaningful.

Pattern Inspiration

Look around you for repeating designs you can transform into a chip carving pattern. This one was inspired by a design on a mirror frame in my home. I created different size chips to add interest and transformed the design elements into shapes that could be chip carved.

Getting Started

Make or purchase a frame sized for the pattern, or adjust the pattern to fit your frame. Sand with 220-grit or finer sandpaper. Remove the dust and secure the pattern to the frame in a few places. Use graphite paper to trace the pattern onto the blank. Alternatively, secure a fresh laser copy of the pattern facedown on the wood and use a heated tool, such as a Pattern Transfer Tool (page 7), to transfer the image to the wood. Make sure your knife is sharp; for a project like this, I prefer a pointed one, such as a diamond modified chip carving knife.

While I'll show you how to carve just one part of this pattern, for maximum efficiency and consistency, make the first cuts on all of the chips across the entire side of the frame. Then make the second cuts, and the third, and so on.

CARVING THE LARGE CURVED CHIPS

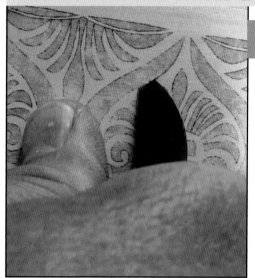

1 **Make the first cut on the inside of one of the large curved chips.** Angle the knife toward the center of the chip. Lock your thumb against the handle of the knife, and place the tip of your thumb and knuckles on the wood to form a 55° to 65° angle with the blade. As the chip gets wider, increase the depth of cut so the point of the knife stays in the center of the chip; this keeps the bottom of the chip precisely in its center. The cuts on this chip make a 360° turn, so remember to turn the frame under the knife (See Smooth Curves, page 38).

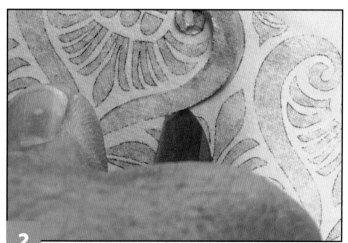

2 **Make the second cut on the outside of the large curved chips.** If both cuts meet in the center (bottom) of the chip, this cut will free it. If the chip doesn't pop free, repeat Step 1 and Step 2 to deepen the cuts. Do not scrape or pry when making these additional cuts to free the chips. Repeat these steps for all of the chips except the ones near the miter joints.

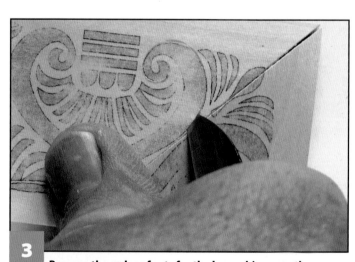

3 **Reverse the order of cuts for the large chips near the corner miter joints.** Make the first cut along the outside of the curve so the knife is angled away from the joint. This will prevent the wood from chipping out along the miter joint. Then cut along the inside of the curve with the knife angled toward the joint. Carve the remaining large curved chips.

CARVING THE INNER FAN

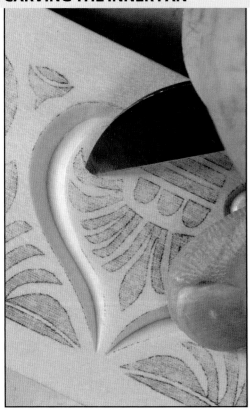

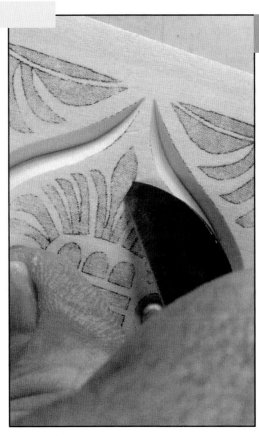

4 **Make all of the cuts along the inside curve on the inner fan section.** Cut from the outside to the center. Right-handed carvers should carve the chips from right to left; left-handed carvers should carve the chips from left to right.

5 **Make the small cuts along the bottom of the chips in the inner fan section.** Righties cut from right to left (or top to bottom, depending on your perspective) while lefties reverse the cuts.

6 **Carve along the outside curves of the inner fan section.** Cut from the bottom of the fan to the top to free the chips. Notice that you are making this final cut starting at the delicate area that often chips out. Following this order of cuts will help prevent annoying chip-out.

SMOOTH CURVES

To chip carve smooth curves, turn the frame underneath the tip of your knife. With practice, you can do this by carving on a smooth lapboard or tabletop. An easier way is to use a large lazy Susan that fully supports your carving. To prevent the lazy Susan from moving as you carve, place a nonslip mat under your work and the lazy Susan. Center the curve being carved and you'll find it easy to turn your work as necessary.

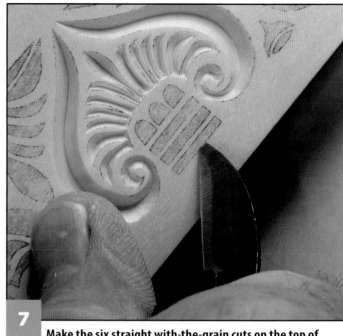

7 **Make the six straight with-the-grain cuts on the top of the design.** Start with the three long cuts for the rectangular chips. Then cut the base of the three tombstone-shaped chips.

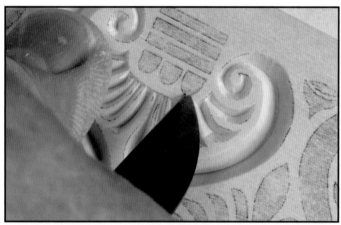

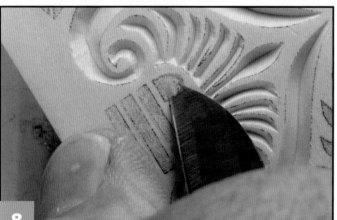

8 **Carve the tombstone-shaped chips.** Insert the knife into the full depth where the side meets the base of the chips. Carefully move the knife up to the top of the tombstone, drawing the knife out until only the tip is in the wood. Rotate the frame to make the curved cut. Then press the knife back into the full depth. This technique gives you a tight, smooth, curved cut.

9 **Make the remaining three cuts with the grain for the rectangular chips.** Then make the across-the-grain cuts on the ends of each rectangle. If all of the cuts meet at the bottom of the chip, you'll hear a snap as the chip pops free. If not, carefully repeat the cuts.

CARVING THE OUTER FAN

 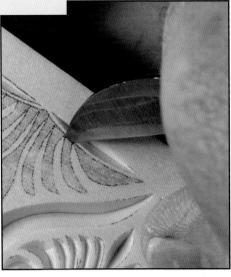 

10 **Carve the first side of the oval chips in the outer fan.** Angle the knife toward the inside of the frame. Make the second cut on the other side to remove the chip. Make one cut along the bottom of the fan rays and continue through the other oval chip. Then carve along the other side of the oval to free that chip.

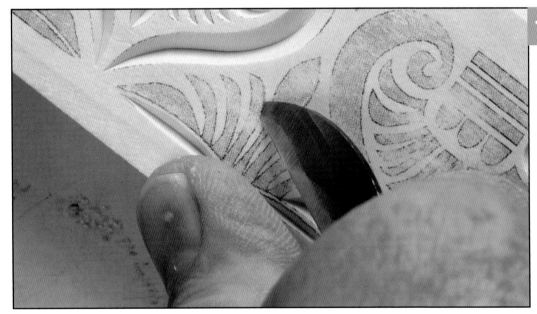

11 **Roll the knife over in your hand as you free the other deep oval chip.** This allows you to cut from a different direction and prevents chip-out in the short grain area between this chip and the adjacent one. Grip the knife as shown in the photo while you make this cut.

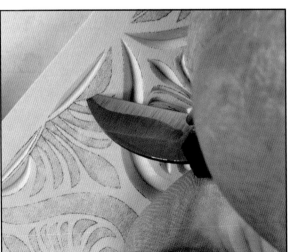 

12 **Starting at the bottom, carve around the outside of the rays of the fan.** Carve toward the top, just like you did on the other fan. By now, if you followed this order of cuts, you should have hardly any chip-out.

Family Photo Frame Pattern

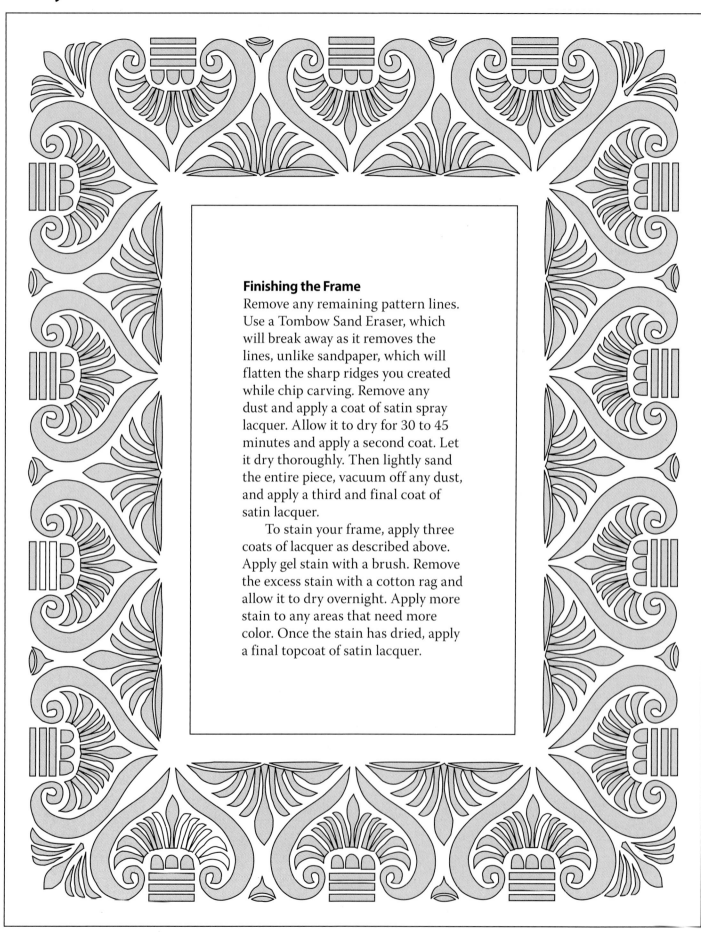

Finishing the Frame

Remove any remaining pattern lines. Use a Tombow Sand Eraser, which will break away as it removes the lines, unlike sandpaper, which will flatten the sharp ridges you created while chip carving. Remove any dust and apply a coat of satin spray lacquer. Allow it to dry for 30 to 45 minutes and apply a second coat. Let it dry thoroughly. Then lightly sand the entire piece, vacuum off any dust, and apply a third and final coat of satin lacquer.

To stain your frame, apply three coats of lacquer as described above. Apply gel stain with a brush. Remove the excess stain with a cotton rag and allow it to dry overnight. Apply more stain to any areas that need more color. Once the stain has dried, apply a final topcoat of satin lacquer.

Rosette Cribbage Board

By Marty Leenhouts

A rosette is a classic design you can use to embellish almost anything, such as a box top, furniture, door, or mantle. Here, we're carving an 8" (20.3cm)-diameter rosette into the center of a cribbage board. (Don't play cribbage? Make a plate or plaque instead.) It's large enough for you to learn the techniques. Then you can increase or reduce the size of the pattern to fit other items.

If you are uncertain about a portion of the pattern, carve it on a practice board before trying it on your project. Practicing first makes for a much more enjoyable and successful chip carving.

Getting Started

Sand the surface with progressively finer grits of sandpaper up to 220-grit. Transfer the pattern to the blank; I use a Pattern Transfer Tool, but you could trace the pattern onto the blank using graphite paper. Cut the perimeter of the blank and drill the peg holes. Or, use a purchased blank.

materials & **tools**

MATERIALS
- Basswood, ¾" (1.9cm) thick: 11½" (29.2cm) square (or precut blank)
- Spray finish: clear satin acrylic or lacquer
- Graphite transfer paper (optional)
- Gel stain: dark mahogany
- Sandpaper: assorted grits up to 220
- Vacuum
- Clean cotton rag
- Tombow Sand Eraser

TOOLS
- Chip carving knife
- Pattern Transfer Tool
- Band saw or scroll saw (optional)
- Drill press with bits: assorted small
- Paintbrush

The author used these products for the project. Substitute your choice of brands, tools, and materials as desired.

CARVING THE ROSETTE

1 **Position your hand in the center of the rosette and work out from there.** That way you don't have to rest your hand on areas you've already carved. Make the first cut on one of the angled lines parallel with the grain. Work around the center of the pattern in a counterclockwise direction so you will make the last cut, adjacent to the first cut, with the grain. Following this order of cuts will help remove the last chip without any chip-out.

2 **Make the four outside cuts around the Gothic leaf shapes.** Then make a cut to remove the majority of one-half of the shape. Finish carving this chip by placing the point in the bottom of the chip as you cut. This cut ensures that the ridge and the valley meet in the center and bottom of the chip. Repeat these same cuts on the other side of the leaf.

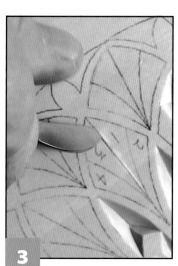
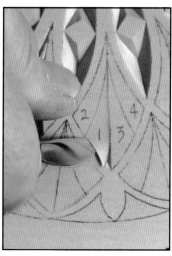
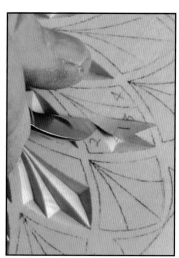
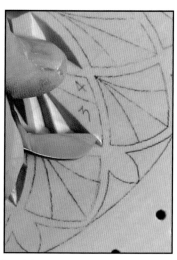

3 **Carve the first of four chips in the fan-shaped designs.** Each chip requires four cuts. There's not necessarily a right or wrong order of cuts on these fan shapes, but I've found success by starting from the centerline and working out on each side of the fan.

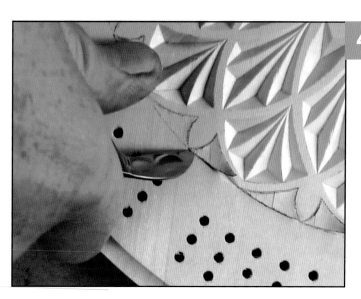

4 **Make the inside cuts on all of the three-corner chips on the outer rim.** To free the chips, make the final cut along the outside line in one continuous, fluid motion. *Note: If you stop and start often on these cuts, the border will look ragged.*

TIP

PREVENT SPLIT CHIPS

Make the first cut on a new chip with the knife angled away from the adjacent chip you just finished. This will prevent the chips from splitting out.

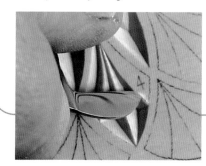

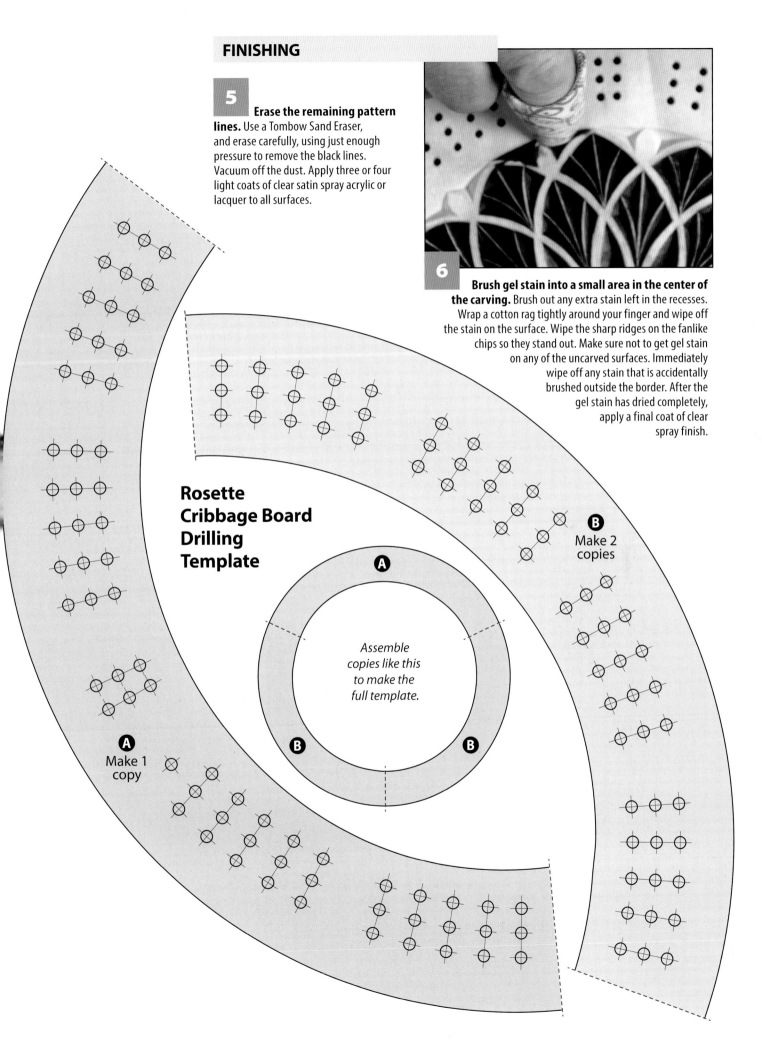

5 **Erase the remaining pattern lines.** Use a Tombow Sand Eraser, and erase carefully, using just enough pressure to remove the black lines. Vacuum off the dust. Apply three or four light coats of clear satin spray acrylic or lacquer to all surfaces.

6 **Brush gel stain into a small area in the center of the carving.** Brush out any extra stain left in the recesses. Wrap a cotton rag tightly around your finger and wipe off the stain on the surface. Wipe the sharp ridges on the fanlike chips so they stand out. Make sure not to get gel stain on any of the uncarved surfaces. Immediately wipe off any stain that is accidentally brushed outside the border. After the gel stain has dried completely, apply a final coat of clear spray finish.

Rosette Cribbage Board Drilling Template

Assemble copies like this to make the full template.

A Make 1 copy

B Make 2 copies

Rosette
Cribbage Board
Pattern

PROJECTS
FOR DINING

Coffee Scoop

By Deanna Cadoret

I became interested in carving when I saw everyday wooden items, such as spoons, stools, and jam spreaders, made beautiful by the addition of chip carving. In today's world of mass-produced wooden trinkets, there is little that deserves the effort of chip carving, so I started carving my own items that could then be decorated. Handmade scoops, such as this one, make wonderful gifts, especially when paired with a bag of gourmet coffee.

This scoop is sized to measure out the correct amount of grounds I need for each pot of coffee. If you prefer stronger coffee, make the bowl a bit larger. Test the amount of grounds the scoop will hold as you hollow out the bowl.

The same technique can be used to make measuring cups. To determine if the measuring cups are accurate, fill a store-bought measuring cup with water or rice to the level you want the wooden measuring cup to hold. As you get close to finishing the bowl, pour the contents from the measuring cup into the carved bowl. Continue hollowing the scoop or measuring cup until it holds all of the contents from the measuring cup.

CARVING THE SPOON

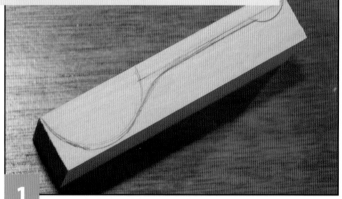

1 **Transfer the scoop pattern.** Slide transfer paper under the pattern and trace the top view and side view of the scoop onto the blank. Be sure to include the inside line of the bowl, but do not transfer the chip carving pattern yet.

2 **Rough out the scoop.** Use a band saw to cut away as much waste wood as possible. Cut 1⁄16" (2mm) outside of the pattern lines. You can also use a sharp knife to rough out the scoop.

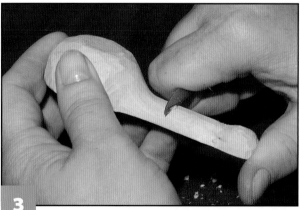

3 **Shape the outside.** Use a knife to remove small amounts of wood from the scoop. Round the bottom of the bowl and carve away the waste outside of the pattern lines. Do not carve away the lines. The lines will be sanded off.

4 **Determine the depth of the bowl.** Drill or carve a 1⁄2" (1.3cm)-diameter by 5⁄8" to 7⁄8" (1.6cm to 2.2cm)-deep hole in the center of the bowl. I used a 1⁄4" (6mm) #5 gouge to carve the hole. Place the tip of the gouge against the wood just off from the center, and spin the gouge around while applying pressure.

materials & **tools**

MATERIALS

- Wood, 1" (2.5cm) thick: 1¾" x 4" (4.4cm x 10.2cm)
- Graphite transfer paper
- Sandpaper: assorted grits up to 600
- Plastic reusable bag (optional)
- Walnut oil or food-safe finish of choice

The author used these products for the project. Substitute your choice of brands, tools, and materials as desired.

TOOLS

- Band saw
- Knives: chip carving, rough out (optional)
- #2 pencil
- #5 gouge: ¼" (6mm)
- Marking instruments

Use the same design on other household items, such as handcarved measuring cups.

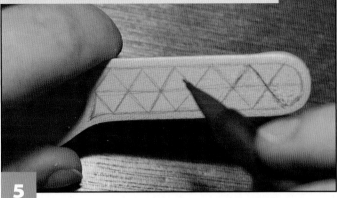

5 **Transfer the chip carving pattern.** Sand the scoop with 80-grit sandpaper to remove all of the gouge and knife marks. Work your way up through the grits to 600 grit for a smooth finish. The more time you spend sanding, the smoother the finished scoop will be. Transfer the chip carving pattern with a #2 pencil and a very light touch.

6 **Finish carving the bowl.** Use the ¼" (6mm) #5 gouge to carve grooves from the inside border of the bowl to the hole carved in the center. Continue cutting grooves until the outer portion of the bowl is as deep as the center hole.

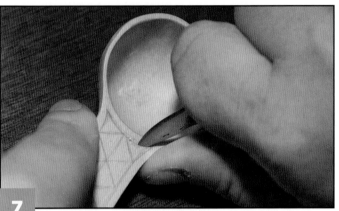

7 **Remove the chips.** Cut along the first line with a chip carving knife. Angle the knife so the deepest part of the cut will be in the center of the triangle. Make the two additional cuts. Maintain the same angle on the knife so all three cuts intersect in the center of the triangle. Use the same technique to carve all of the remaining chips.

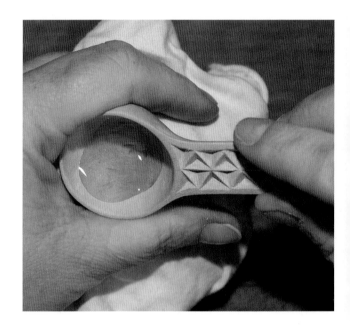

Coffee Scoop Pattern

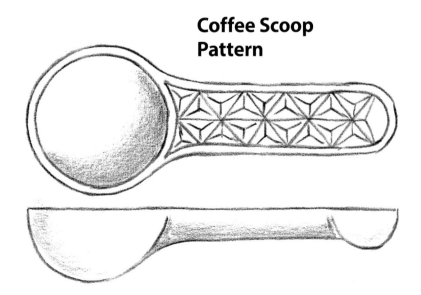

Finishing

Pour about ½ teaspoon (2.5mL) of walnut oil into the bowl and rotate the scoop gently to coat the entire inside of the bowl. Pour the excess oil out. Drip a small amount of oil onto the end of the handle and hold the scoop at a slight incline so the oil fills each chip. Add more oil as needed. Use your finger to apply oil to the back of the scoop. Apply two to three coats of oil, allowing each coat to dry for 24 hours before applying the next.

For a deep penetrating finish, place the scoop and ¼ cup (59mL) of walnut oil into a plastic resealable bag. Remove as much air as possible and seal the bag. Turn the bag every day for three days. The oil will soak deep into the wood, bringing out the grain, and the oil can be saved for another project. Then store the scoop in coffee grounds. The oils from the coffee will slowly color the scoop.

Summery Supernova Coasters

By Roman Chernikov

If you have avoided chip carving till now because it's too intimidating, then my supernova coasters, inspired by the look of an exploding star, are an ideal first project. In these patterns, I placed the chips farther apart than usual, so no two share the same edge; this virtually eliminates the common mistakes that lead to broken or uneven ridges.

materials & **tools**

MATERIALS
- Basswood, at least ¼" (6mm) thick: 4" (10.2cm) square
- Graphite transfer paper
- Pencil
- Sandpaper: 220-grit
- Finish: clear acrylic spray

The author used these products for the project. Substitute your choice of brands, tools, and materials as desired.

TOOLS
- Chip carving knife
- Hot tool (to transfer pattern, optional)

Supernova Coaster Patterns

Making the Coasters

Cut the blanks to size and sand them smooth using 220-grit sandpaper. Round the edges if desired. Transfer the patterns to the blanks using a hot tool with a laser print or graphite transfer paper. Strop your knife before you begin carving the chips.

I use simple three-corner chips with straight edges to carve the supernovas, which consist of 108 chips each. Refer to the photos to keep track of where the deepest part of the chip should be. Once you've carved the coasters, apply several light coats of acrylic spray finish, letting the entire piece dry between coats.

TIP

PRACTICE, PRACTICE, PRACTICE

Making rosettes is the best way to learn carving with the grain, as the chips align with the grain at many different angles. Carve a rosette or two on a practice board before starting your project.

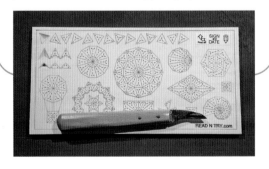

Simple Cereal Bowl

By Amy Costello

As a turner and chip carver, I'm always looking for new ways to combine these skills in interesting ways. After gluing a basswood stripe for carving into a cribbage board I made for my dad, I was inspired to add a similar stripe to a set of cereal bowls. While carving, do your best to cut each facet with a single stroke; lots of practice and a razor-sharp tool are key!

materials & tools

MATERIALS

All wood dimensions refer to the size of the blank, not the finished bowl

- Walnut or cherry, 2½" (6.4cm) thick: 6½" (16.5cm) square
- Walnut or cherry, ½" (1.3cm) thick: 6½" (16.5cm) square
- Basswood, ¾" (1.9cm) thick: approx. 2" x 18" (5.1cm x 45.7cm)
- Pencil
- Wood glue
- Sandpaper: assorted grits up to 500
- Clear finish, such as Odie's® Oil and natural Danish oil
- Clean cotton cloths

TOOLS

- Saws: table, miter
- Chip carving knife
- Midi-lathe with assorted turning tools
- Ruler: flexible cloth
- Clamps (or vise)

The author used these products for the project. Substitute your choice of brands, tools, and materials as desired.

Preparing the Blanks

Carving on bowls comes with its own set of challenges. The biggest issue is that most bowls are turned with the grain running horizontally. This makes for stronger bowls, but it also means that at least half of the carving surface is end grain or similar. End grain is a pain to carve, and I was never quite satisfied with the results I got from simply gluing a rectangle of basswood onto a regular bowl blank. Luckily, the turning world already had an elegant solution that allowed me to create a continuous edge grain surface around the entire bowl. It's called segmenting—gluing several smaller pieces together to form a larger blank.

Make your blanks. With segmenting, you can control the orientation of each piece, allowing you to create blanks with ideal grain configuration that would otherwise be impossible to achieve. For my bowls, I made basswood hexagons (basically picture frames with 30° miters instead of 45°) using a miter saw. (Find a template of the hexagon glueup below.) Then I resawed a thick chunk

of walnut on the band saw, jointed the inside faces, and sandwiched the basswood hexagon between them, clamping the blank tightly. It's important that the glue joint between every piece of the blank is extremely tight; otherwise, you'll end up with hairline holes in your bowl! Let the glue dry and remove the clamps.

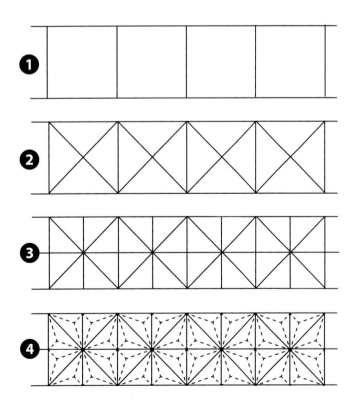

Simple Cereal Bowl Patterns

Hexagon Section
Cut 6

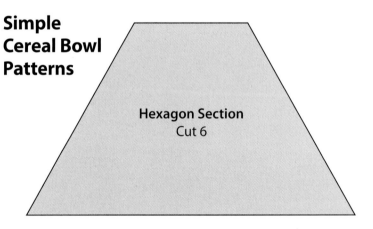

Scale up the blank to make larger serving bowls, if desired.

1 **Turn the bowl.** I turn mine until the circumference at the basswood stripe can be split evenly into round numbers when divided by ¾. Measure using a flexible cloth ruler. Once you've achieved the size you want, sand with 150-grit sandpaper, and then sand progressively through the grits until you reach 500. Apply a natural finish of your choice to the portion that will remain uncarved; leave the outside of the basswood stripe unfinished for now. *Note: I typically sand and finish the bowl while it's on the lathe, so I can take advantage of the friction-finish properties of Odie's Oil, my favorite finish for bowls.*

2 **Apply the pattern to the basswood stripe.** When you're ready to carve, lay out a row of squares that is approximately the same width as the basswood stripe. (I say approximately because it's more important that the circumference of the bowl is divided up evenly than that the pattern is made of perfect squares.) Then draw the diagonals by connecting the corners of each square. Use the center point those diagonals created to mark the vertical and horizontal axis of each square. Then secure the bowl with clamps or a vise so it doesn't wiggle loose during carving.

3 **Carve the bowl.** If you're proficient in Swiss-style chip carving, use the layout from Figure 3 (page 52) in the pattern to begin. If you're a beginner, you might try English-style chip carving, which is my preferred method. If you chose the latter, begin by making relief cuts along the dotted lines in Figure 4 (page 52). The deepest part of each relief cut will share a point in the center of each inverted pyramid shape, becoming shallower at the edges. Once you've made a relief cut along each of the dotted lines, you can start removing chips as you would with Swiss-style carving. Work through the rest of the three-corner chips, adjusting the bowl position and vise as necessary until the carving is complete.

4 **Finish the bowl.** I don't sand after carving due to the risk of accidentally softening the crisp edges of the cuts. Apply a natural finish to the carved stripe; I like to use a penetrating oil, such as Danish oil, but any finish that won't pool up on the surface will work. Wipe off the excess with a clean cotton cloth and let dry.

Afternoon Tea Caddy

By Marty Leenhouts

Tea is the second most widely consumed drink around the world, after water. If you aren't a tea drinker, you surely know someone who is. Storing several varieties of tea separately in the cupboard is messy and takes up a lot of space, as well as making it challenging to offer the assortment to guests. Chip carve a premade box to neatly organize tea bags in eight compartments, creating a unique way to store and serve this common drink.

The design is a positive image design, meaning that you will remove the background, shown in gray, so the leaves remain proud on the surface. The depths of the cuts will vary with the width of the chips.

Getting Started

Remove the clasp so you can sand the entire box with progressively finer grits of paper through at least 220-grit. Remove the dust with a vacuum. Use a photocopier to resize the pattern to fit your box if necessary. The pattern is designed for transferring with graphite paper. However, I use a hot Pattern Transfer Tool with a toner-based laser print.

Some fonts are easier to carve than others; the rounded ends of the one I chose are challenging to carve but look distinctive when completed. If desired, choose and size a different font using a word processor. I suggest you practice carving the letters before carving the box. Transfer the letters to the box using the method of your choice.

materials & **tools**

MATERIALS
- Basswood box
- Graphite transfer paper (optional)
- Eraser, such as Tombow Sand Eraser
- Sanding sealer
- Lacquer: spray satin
- Gel stain

TOOLS
- Chip carving knife
- Pattern Transfer Tool
- Masking tape

The author used these products for the project. Substitute your choice of brands, tools, and materials as desired.

CARVING THE LEAVES

1 **Carve the outer line of the box lid.** Stack boards or books alongside the box to provide a base for your hand so you can maintain the proper grip, hand, and arm position to carve precise chips. Try to make one continuous cut whenever possible. This will create smooth lines and avoid stop-start marks.

2 **Remove the large chips.** It is helpful to carve a smaller chip from the center first. Then go back and carve along the outer and inner lines to free the large chip cleanly.

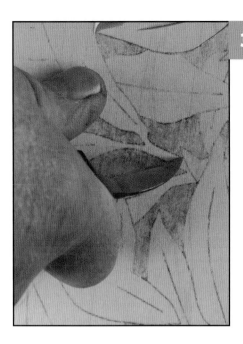

3 **Carve the inner leaves.** Determine the grain direction before you begin (see Tip, at right). Start a cut at the base of the leaf and continue until the cut runs into another overlapping leaf. When carving the lines where leaves overlap, vary the width of the chips (which will also vary the depth of the chips) to add variety and interest to your carving. Rotate the box as needed. Notice how the third cut removed the chip cleanly because it was cut with the grain. Roll the knife (see Tip) as needed to remove the adjacent chips.

(see Tip, at right)

TIP

DETERMINING GRAIN DIRECTION

When removing chips, make as many cuts as possible with the grain. I use a deck of cards to help determine the proper direction. Place the deck in line with the grain along the outside edge of the cut. Then angle the edge of the cards along the pattern line. The edge of the cards will ripple smoothly in just one direction—with the grain. To cut along the grain and free the chip in this area, roll the knife and place your thumb under the handle so it remains on the wood to form a stable base and consistent angle.

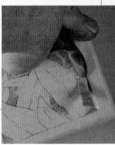

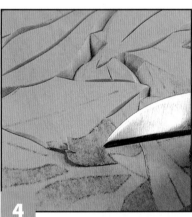
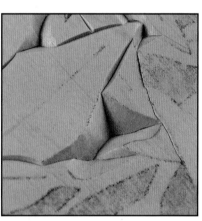

4 **Start cuts in the waste when possible.** That way, the cut extends down into the bottom of the chip in the middle of the background area. Repeat this general process to remove the remaining background around the leaves.

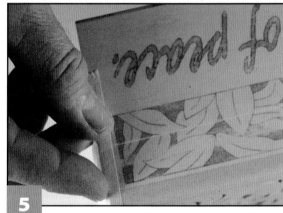

5 **Carve the leaves on the front and sides of the box.** Apply strips of masking tape to keep the box closed, and carve as you would if the box were a solid piece of wood. Be careful when removing chips that extend across the top and bottom sections of the box.

CARVING THE LETTERS

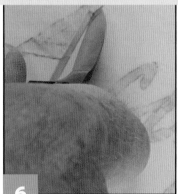

6 **Carve the main section of the capital A.** Start the inside cut just above the peak of the inner triangle. Make the outer cut starting at the top of the letter. If you don't start the cut just past the peak of the inner triangle, you will end up with some uncut wood, which leaves fuzzies in the bottom of the cut.

7 **Carve along the outsides of the curved letters.** As you approach the tight curve at the end of each letter, rotate the box under the point of the knife. At the top of the curve, draw all but the tip of the knife out of the top of the wood. The small tip of the knife allows you to cut cleanly along the curve.

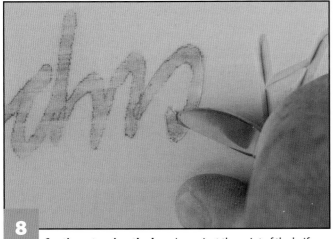

8 **Continue turning the box.** Leave just the point of the knife in the wood. As you pass the tight part, press the knife back into the wood to create depth and free the chip. This technique allows you to carve the rounded ends of the letters.

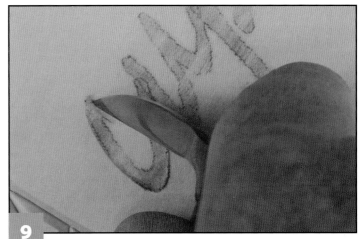

9 **Place the tip of the knife at the bottom of the chip you just freed.** This starting point ensures that all of the cuts meet in the exact same place. Start carving at this point and work smoothly around the inside of the letter.

10 **Erase any remaining pattern lines.** I use a Tombow Sand Eraser, which removes the dark lines but breaks down as it erases so it will not damage the carved surfaces.

Sanding and Finishing

Apply a coat of sanding sealer. Remove any raised grain or rough spots, and then apply a coat of spray satin lacquer. Let the lacquer dry, and then apply a coat of gel stain to darken the carved recesses. Allow the gel stain to dry overnight, and apply a final coat of spray satin lacquer.

Afternoon Tea Caddy Pattern *(side)*

Size this pattern to fit your box.

Afternoon Tea Caddy Patterns
(box front and lid)

Size these patterns to fit your box.

A cup of tea is a cup of peace.

PROJECTS FOR DRESSING

Stylish Combs

By Roman and Olga Repikova

Natural materials impart a feeling of comfort and bring us closer to the earth. When creating these beard and hair combs, follow two basic rules—practicality and simplicity of design. If you choose an attractive hardwood, make sure to orient the grain so that it flows in the same direction as the teeth; otherwise, they will easily snap. Stack and glue together multiple layers of ash veneer for the folding hair comb to ensure durability.

materials & **tools**

MATERIALS

- Walnut, ¼" (6mm) thick: beard comb, sized for pattern
- Alder, ⅜" (1cm) thick: folding comb case bottom, sized for pattern
- Alder, ⅛" (3mm) thick: folding comb case top, sized for pattern
- Ash veneer, layered to ⅛" (3mm) thick: folding comb, sized for pattern
- Wood glue
- Tape: blue painter's
- Spray adhesive
- Sandpaper: assorted grits up to 220
- Pivot pin, ¼" (6mm)-dia.: ½" (1.3cm) long
- Oil-based stain, such as walnut
- Turpentine oil
- Beeswax
- Essential oil (optional)

TOOLS

- Scroll saw with blades: #3 reverse-tooth
- CNC machine (optional)
- Chip carving knife
- Drill with bits: assorted small
- #5 gouge: ¼" (6mm)
- #9 gouge: ⅛" (3mm)
- Brush: medium-to-coarse
- Clamps: small

The author used these products for the project. Substitute your choice of brands, tools, and materials as desired.

Getting Started

Sand down the wood pieces and cover them with blue painter's tape. Photocopy the patterns and attach them to the wood with spray adhesive. We used a CNC machine to cut out the comb blanks, but you can use a scroll saw with a #3 reverse-tooth blade. Drill the holes for the pivot pin in the folding comb and case pieces.

A stylish comb to tame the wildest of beards and a folding hair comb perfect for storing in a purse or pack.

Stylish Comb Patterns

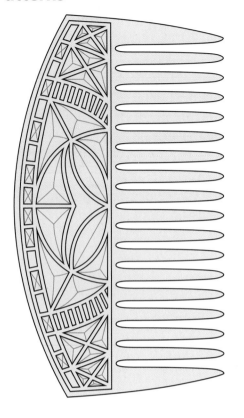

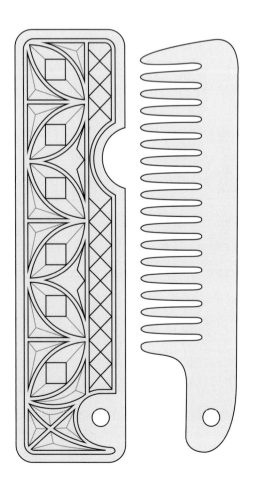

Assembling and Carving

Dry-assemble the hair comb and case to make sure the comb will fit inside the slot. Then glue the top and bottom of the case together, clamp, and let dry. Once dry, sand off any sharp corners.

Carve the beard comb and hair comb case. Start with the chip carving knife, referring to the patterns as you create two-, three-, and four-corner chips. Then use a ¼" (6mm) #5 gouge to carve the borders around the leaves and the perimeter of each design; use a ⅛" (3mm) #9 gouge for the feathering on the beard comb.

Sanding and Finishing

Once you've carved the beard comb and folding comb case, gently sand the combs to 220-grit so that, on a side view, the teeth taper almost to a point. Cover all of the pieces with walnut stain. Allow the stain to dry, and then sand them again. This will remove the stain from the flat surfaces and allow it to remain in the carved chips, adding contrast to the finished combs.

Finish the combs with beeswax dissolved in turpentine oil; this gives them a beautiful shine and a unique aroma. Feel free to add a few drops of your preferred essential oil to the mixture for a personal touch. After coating the pieces, allow a little time for the wood to soak up the mixture, and then rub with a medium-to-coarse brush. Add the folding comb and pivot pin to the case.

Homemade Knife

Roman designed this knife to carve geometric patterns and reliefs. It has a thin, sharp carbon steel blade, which is shaped to allow us to cut both toward and away from ourselves in a few fluid motions. It has a comfortable walnut handle finished with raw natural linseed oil, and works well for both soft and hard wood.

Aloe Leaf Earrings

By Amy Costello

In an effort to improve my skills, I challenged myself to design and carve a new pattern every week for these wooden hoop earrings. I arrived at this particular design while playing around with a compass. I developed the curved diamond pattern by overlapping two sets of concentric circles: one centered at the top of the big hole and the other centered at the bottom. To lay out the aloe leaves, I then drew smooth curves from certain intersections of those circles to a shared point at the bottom of the earring.

This set makes for a perfect stocking stuffer around the holidays. You can prepare a bunch of blanks at once and then carve a handful in a sitting. The milk paint adds a nice accent without stealing the show; mix up whichever colors you prefer and go to town!

materials & **tools**

MATERIALS

- Basswood, ¼" (6mm) thick: 2 each approx. 2¾" (7cm) square
- Sandpaper: assorted grits from 150 to 320
- Graphite transfer paper (optional)
- Pencil (optional)
- Milk paint: light green
- Finish, such as clear spray lacquer
- Metal earring hooks: 2 each
- Jump rings, ¼" (6mm): 2 each

TOOLS

- Scroll saw with #3 reverse-tooth blades, band saw, or midi-lathe with assorted chisels
- Chip carving knife, such as Pfeil #2
- Drill with bits: 1" (25mm)-dia. Forstner, 1/16" (2mm)-dia.
- Sander: pneumatic drum (optional)
- Paintbrushes: assorted small

The author used these products for the project. Substitute your choice of brands, tools, and materials as desired.

Getting Started

I made the blanks for these earrings by turning them on a lathe, but you could also make them with a band saw or scroll saw. If you use a lathe, start by boring the center hole with a Forstner bit, and then mount the drilled blank on a chuck with an off-center tenon that matches the hole with a snug friction fit. I like using the lathe because it allows me to make a perfectly round outer edge and dome the face of the earring quickly.

If you decide to use a band saw or scroll saw, transfer the pattern using your preferred method; I recommend graphite paper and a pencil. Drill the central hole and then carefully cut the perimeters. Dome the surface slightly using an orbital sander. Make sure your blanks are thin enough to be comfortable to wear, but thick enough that they won't disintegrate during carving. Drill the small holes for the findings and you're ready to go!

Carving and Finishing

Sand the blanks, moving up progressively through the grits from 150 to 320. To carve each chip in the English style (my preferred method), start by making relief or stop cuts that follow what will become the low edges of each diamond and lozenge shape. *Note: These cuts are represented by the dotted lines on the pattern.* Then make slicing cuts along each facet—as you would with Swiss-style chip carving—moving from the high edges down to converge at the lowest point and remove the waste material. *Note: These cuts are represented by the solid lines on the pattern.* Aim for clean cuts straight off the knife, because any sanding after the fact will dull the crisp edges that make chip carving so beautiful. Take extra care with the round inside and outside borders. The earrings should be 2¼" (5.7cm) round when finished. Scale them down if you wish.

Once the carving is complete, paint the aloe leaves carefully with a small brush. Take your time. If you accidentally get paint somewhere you shouldn't, wait for it to dry before slicing it off with a sharp knife. I paint the backs of these earrings as well as the edges and leaves. When the paint is dry, finish with a clear coat of spray-on lacquer, and then add the metal findings.

Aloe Leaf Earring Pattern

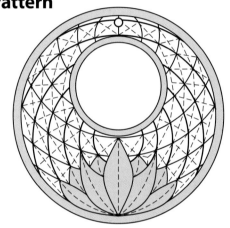

Keepsake Box

By Tom Noller

A s a chip carver, when I look at something made of wood, I immediately imagine how I can embellish it. When I attended a demonstration on making band saw boxes, I realized I can make them of any shape. I enjoy making simple keepsake boxes, like this one, because there is no complex joinery required to build them.

Getting Started

I used a band saw with a ¼" (6mm)-wide, 6-tooth-per-inch (tpi) blade and a scroll saw with a #9 blade. You can make your box almost any width, but the thickness is limited to what you can cut with a scroll saw or coping saw (approximately 2", or 5.1cm). If you use a band saw to cut the center of the box, you'll need to cut a separate lid liner. Just trace the interior of the box sides onto ³⁄₁₆" (5mm)-thick wood and cut it out.

It's easy to adapt this idea to different chip carving patterns—just trace a box shape around the chip design and cut it as shown here. I've added some bonus patterns on page 67. If the box is unstable on its side, temporarily attach it to a square board when you slice off the top and bottom for safety.

materials & **tools**

MATERIALS
- Basswood, 2" (5.1cm) thick: 3½" x 5½" (8.9cm x 14cm)
- Sandpaper: 220-grit
- Wood glue
- Stain, such as Minwax® golden pecan
- Finish: clear spray
- Flocking (optional)

TOOLS
- Band saw with blade: ¼" (6mm) wide (6tpi)
- Drill with bit: ¹⁄₁₆" (2mm)
- Scroll saw with blades: #9 reverse-tooth
- Chip carving knife
- Clamps: small

The author used these products for the project. Substitute your choice of brands, tools, and materials as desired.

MAKING THE BOX

1 **Attach the pattern to the blank.** Cut the perimeter with a band saw. Rip a ⅛" (3mm)-thick slice from the bottom. Rip a ¼" (6mm)-thick slice off the top. Mark the top and bottom of the center section.

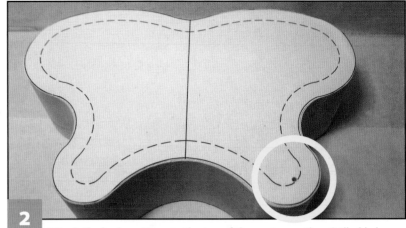

2 **Attach the body pattern to the top of the center section.** Drill a blade-entry hole just inside the inner line. Insert a scroll saw or coping saw blade and cut the center. Go slowly and let the blade do the work. *Note: This wood is thick and will take time to cut.* Mark the top and bottom of the box sides and the cutout.

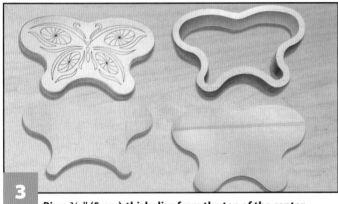

3 **Rip a ³⁄₁₆" (5mm)-thick slice from the top of the center cutout.** Use the band saw. This will be the lid liner. Depending on the size of your box, you might be able to use what remains of this center section to make another box.

4 **Glue the slice you cut in Step 3 to the inside of the top.** Use the body of the box to center it in place. You need to have a slight space all around the insert so the top will sit comfortably without getting stuck. Carefully remove the body and clamp the insert to the top without moving it. Don't use too much glue or it will tend to slide. Wipe away any squeeze-out so it will not interfere with the top fitting.

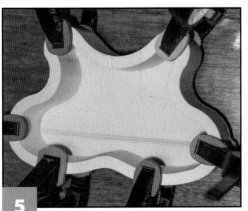

5 **Sand the inside of the box sides and the top of the bottom.** Then glue and clamp the bottom to the sides. Remove any squeeze-out from the inside of the body. Check the fit of the top, and sand the top and bottom with 220-grit sandpaper.

CARVING THE DESIGN

6 **Transfer the chip carving pattern to the top.** Carve the chips. Then finish the box. I used Minwax golden pecan stain. When the stain is dry, apply a clear spray finish. Add flocking to the inside of the box if desired.

Keepsake Box Patterns

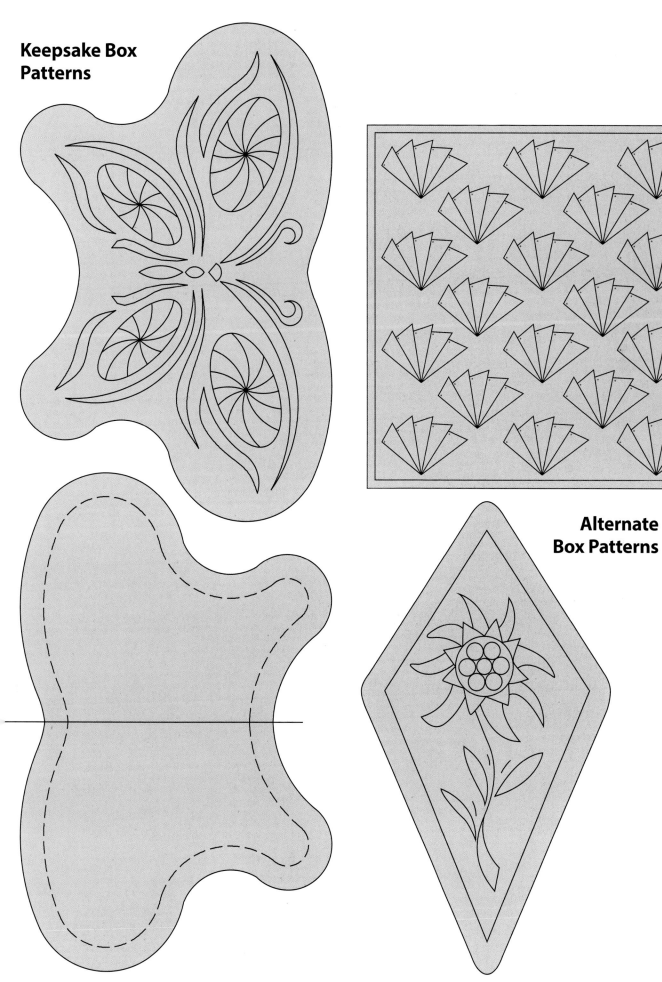

Alternate Box Patterns

Milk Paint Jewelry Box

By Tatiana Baldina

Creating patterns has become a special process for me. Each of the nearly 1,000 patterns I have created since I began chip carving six years ago is a combination of my emotions and experiences. I believe that the impact of a pattern is largely dependent on how the design is bound within a given space. In this project, the pattern I used organically led to different choices about colors, shapes, and finishing techniques. All of the elements are thoughtfully planned out—and only require a few tools to tie together.

Getting Started

Assemble the box, or use a prepurchased one that measures roughly 3⅝" (9.2cm) square and 2¼" (5.7cm) high. If making the box from scratch, refer to the Parts List on page 72. Photocopy the patterns (except the top semicircle on the sides of the box—you'll do that later) and transfer them to the box elements using your preferred method. I sketched mine on, but you could also use graphite paper and a pencil or ballpoint pen. I will show you how to carve the entire pattern by demonstrating how to complete just one quarter; you can apply the same method to the rest of the carving. Practice your first few cuts on a piece of scrap wood until you are confident.

CARVING THE TOP

1 Make stop cuts inside all the long four-corner chips. Start with the long stop cut along the center of each chip, digging the blade approximately ⅛" (3mm) deep. Then carve the two remaining central cuts in each four-corner chip. Undercut each of the four facets at a 60° angle.

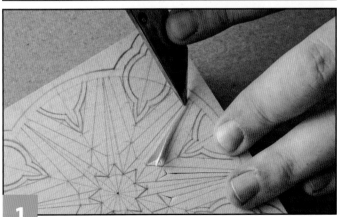

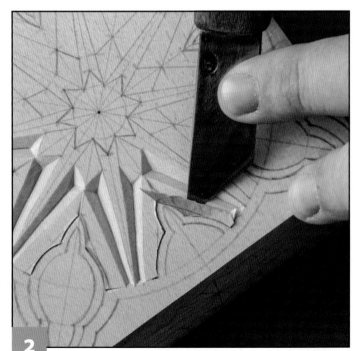

2 Carve the perimeter shapes. Following the shapes of the dart figures, cut at a nearly 90° angle, as if for a straight-wall chip. Then come in from the outer perimeter of each dart, relieving the border at a roughly 60° angle. Try to complete each facet in one cut for a clean, continuous surface.

Undercutting

One of the main challenges for beginners is that when you have not developed muscle memory around certain techniques, it's hard to understand how deeply you should undercut a facet. A beginner chip carver will often push the knife in too far. I suggest practicing before you begin the project: draw several triangles of different sizes on a piece of scrap wood identical to the material for your project. Make stop cuts inside each of them, and then start to undercut the facets slightly—one by one—until they pop out. Soon, you will get a feel for how much pressure is required in each cut.

MATERIALS

- Basswood, ³⁄₈" (1cm) thick: practice top, 3⅝" (9.2cm) square; practice side, 1¾" x 3⅝" (4.4cm x 9.2cm)
- Basswood, ³⁄₈" (1cm) thick: sides, feet, and top (see Parts List)
- Basswood, ⅛" (3mm) thick: bottom, 3⅝" (9.2cm) square
- Graphite transfer paper
- Pencil: HB standard
- Eraser
- Wood dowel, ⅛" (3mm)-dia.: 1" (2.5cm) long
- Wood glue
- Hinges: 2 each, small

The author used these products for the project. Substitute your choice of brands, tools, and materials as desired.

- Sandpaper: 220-1600 grits
- Danish oil: natural
- Milk paint, such as Miss Mustard Seed's General Finishes: dark chocolate
- Disposable cup

TOOLS

- Table saw
- Miter saw
- Chip carving knife: skew
- Drill with bit: ⅛" (3mm)-dia.
- Soft toothbrush
- Paintbrush: synthetic
- Clamps: small

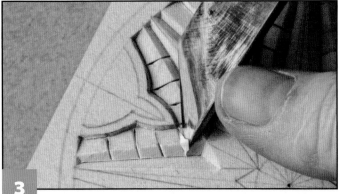

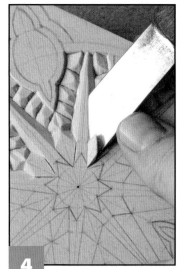

3 **Draw the "peas."** With a pencil, divide the V shapes (those surrounding each dart you just carved) into equal segments. Follow these lines with stop cuts perpendicular to the surface of the lid. Then gently—using only the tip of the knife—round the peas into the deepest areas in the center of the four-corner chips and the edge of the straight-wall chips from Step 2. The deepest cuts will occur on the sides of the peas. When you are done, it will look as though you have split each pea into four facets. Be sure not to add unwanted knife marks to any of the carved facets surrounding the peas. If this does occur, carefully remove the marks right away, as this task will be difficult once all elements are carved.

4 **Define the top of each V.** Make cuts on the inner sides of the rhombuses at an angle of almost 90°; the deepest areas will touch the central star. Then, by placing the knife parallel to one of the sides of the rhombus that faces the star, gently slice off a chip as illustrated. In every other rhombus, make additional decorative slices as shown in the second image.

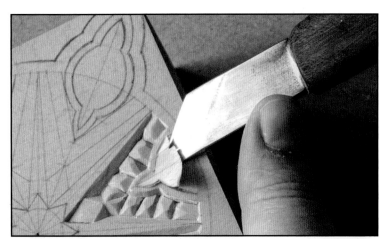

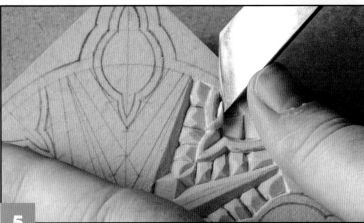

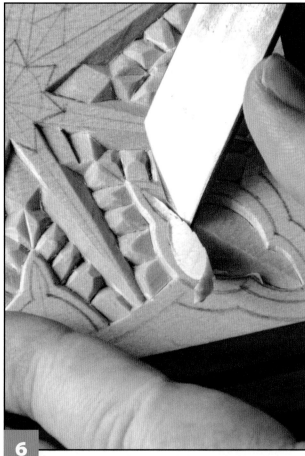

5 **Carve the insides of the four non-corner darts.** Follow the inner border lines at an angle of almost 90°, and then carve in toward those lines, keeping the blade low to the surface of the wood. If the chip does not pop out, repeat all your cuts one more time. To add another layer to these chips, carve two more straight-walled chips inside the central section of the dart. Then undercut them to make the central shape protrude.

6 **Carve the insides of the four corner darts.** Follow the inner border lines at an angle of almost 90°, and then carve into them at an almost 80° angle from the center of the dart to create two large, angled facets. Then, at almost a 90° angle, carve the outer border lines that point toward each corner. Carve in toward those lines at a 60° angle.

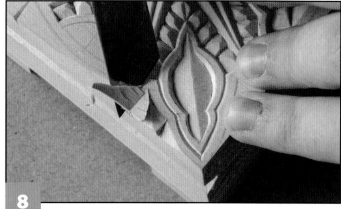

7 **Carve the rays of the star.** Make stop cuts along the center of each ray—one long and two short. Starting at the thinnest outer point, carve inward to remove the first facet in one pass. Do the same for the second. Carve at a 45° angle. Then, at a 60° angle, carve a series of two-corner chips leading in toward the very center of the star.

8 **Add the edge embellishments.** Make deep cuts on the box edge that follow the lines of the darts. Your deepest cut will be around 5⁄16" (8mm) deep. Be particularly careful at this stage; start by making V-shaped cuts and then round them slightly, so the outer "frame" of the lid has a flowy effect.

PAINTING & CARVING THE SIDES

9 **Pour a small amount of dark chocolate milk paint into a disposable cup.** Add a few drops of water and begin to mix the paint, gradually adding water until you reach the consistency of heavy cream. Then apply paint to the surface of the sides where indicated in the photo, leaving the bottom semicircle unpainted. Do the same for the feet. You will need to apply several layers to achieve full opacity. Let dry and then apply the chip carving patterns to the sides using the same method as in Getting Started.

10 **Carve the unpainted sides of each box side.** Follow the same method as on the top. Then carve the top semicircle, starting by cutting the straight chips that radiate out from the center of the circle. Carve the three-corner chips around the perimeter of the top semicircle. Add small angled cuts 1⁄16" (2mm) to 1⁄8" (3mm) in from the right edge of each star point. Cut at a 60° angle, starting from the top.

11 **Carve the bottom semicircle.** Start with the outer cuts, carving at a 35° angle. Then make the same two cuts on the facets inside each of the triangles as you did on the top semicircle. Clean up any messy cuts.

Parts List

Item	Quantity	Basswood	Dimensions
Lid sides	4	⅜" (1cm) thick	15⁄16" x 3⅝" (2.4cm x 9.2cm)
Lid top	1	⅜" (1cm) thick	3⅝" (9.2cm) square
Box sides	4	⅜" (1cm) thick	1¹⁄16" x 3⅝" (2.7cm x 9.2cm)
Box bottom	1	⅛" (3mm) thick	3⅝" (9.2cm) square
Feet	2, cut diagonally into 4	⅜" (1cm) thick	13⁄16" (2.1cm) square

Finishing

Remove the pencil lines with an eraser. For stubborn lines, carefully sand them away with a fine-grit sandpaper.

Apply a finish. I used Danish oil without any stain because I did not want to level out the contrast created by the dark milk paint. If desired, though, you could follow an alternate finishing method, which I outline in the sidebar below.

The Oil-and-Stain Method

I have always wanted to find a variety of finish that enhances the beauty of a carving without hiding any intricate details. After experimenting with Danish oil for the past few years, I have developed a method of application that works well for projects in need of a more dramatic coloring.

First layer: Apply Danish oil without any stain. This layer prepares the wood grain and carved surface for the next layers of oil. Before adding the next layer of oil, brush the carved surface with a clean, soft toothbrush. I do not typically use sandpaper at this stage.

Second layer: Apply a layer of Danish oil mixed with a small amount of your preferred stain.

Third layer: Apply another layer of Danish oil and stain.

Fourth and final layer: Apply a layer of Danish oil without any stain. Let sit for a few minutes and wipe out any excess from the carved areas before it pools.

Milk Paint Jewelry Box Patterns

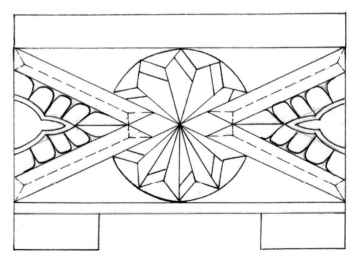

Trio of Barrettes

By Steve Reed

A couple of years ago, I was looking for a Valentine's Day gift for my lovely wife and found some barrette blanks at a carving show. She has long hair, and I thought they would be perfect. I chip carved a barrette for her and she was thrilled. Her friends loved them, too; since then, I've made about 50 barrettes for gifts and local craft shows.

Preparing the Blank

Begin by sanding the barrette blank with a 400-grit sanding block to freshen the surface and make it very smooth.

I draw the pattern directly onto the wood rather than carving through paper or using a transfer tool. Use a 0.5mm mechanical pencil and make light lines so you don't dent the blank with the lead. Using a flexible ruler, find the center of the barrette horizontally and vertically to determine the center point of the piece. Draw a horizontal line through the center to the length of the pattern. You can use a compass to create a rosette in the center or multiple rosettes along the length. For triangular or other geometric chips, I find it simpler to measure in millimeters instead of fractions. A drafting square, such as Rotring's Centro Geo Set Square, makes it easy to determine the center point between two lines.

materials & **tools**

MATERIALS
- Barrette blank: 1⅞" x 4" (4.8cm x 10.2cm) or 1⅞" x 4½" (4.8cm x 11.4cm)
- Sanding block: 400-grit
- Sanding pad, such as Scotch-Brite™: maroon
- Finish: semigloss
- Gel stain: dark
- Tack cloth
- Acrylic paints: assorted (optional)
- Glue: cyanoacrylate (CA)
- Mechanical pencil: 0.5mm
- Eraser: white polymer
- French barrette style hair clips

TOOLS
- Knives: chip carving, stab
- Drafting square, such as Rotring's Centro Geo Set Square (optional)
- Flexible ruler
- Compass (optional)

The author used these products for the project. Substitute your choice of brands, tools, and materials as desired.

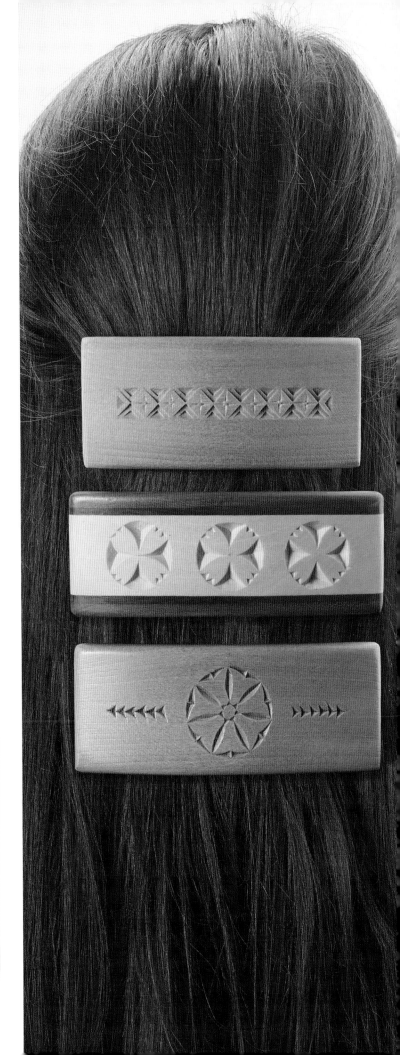

Embellishing with a Stab Knife

I make most of the cuts with a standard chip carving knife. However, in the center of the diamonds on the old-world-style barrette, I used a stab knife to carve simple crosses. Simply press the stab knife in to carve each of the four cuts branching out from the center.

Carving Swiss-Style Chips

For Swiss-style chips (rosettes, organic forms, and geometric chips), the deepest part of the chip is usually in the center. No matter how many sides the chips have, hold the knife at the same angle as you cut the sides of the chip so the cuts meet in the center. For rosettes, make the deepest cuts first, removing the area between the petals. Once you remove the wood around all four petals, carve the small triangles at the ends of the petals.

To keep from breaking a nearby chip, always start a new chip with the knife blade angled away from the just-carved chip. To keep from carving yourself into a corner, start at one end of the line and work your way to the other end. That way, you won't need to carve a chip centered between two already-carved chips.

Sanding and Finishing

Erase any pattern lines with a white polymer eraser. Don't rub too hard, as you can damage the delicate points of the design. Lightly sand the project with the 400-grit sanding block to remove any extra marks or finger smudges. Spray the barrette with at least two coats of semigloss finish. Use a maroon Scotch-Brite™ pad to smooth the piece, and then remove any dust with a tack cloth. Spray on another coat or two of semigloss finish. To make the chips stand out, apply a dark gel stain and immediately wipe it off. The stain will settle into the chips to make them slightly darker than the surface. Be careful—if the project isn't sealed well, the stain can bleed.

If you prefer, before carving the barrette, paint it with full-strength acrylic or craft paint, and then carve the design through the paint. This works especially well with holiday designs (painted red or green) or designs inspired by Asian lacquerware (painted black). Glue on your chosen hardware. Let dry.

Trio of Barrettes Patterns

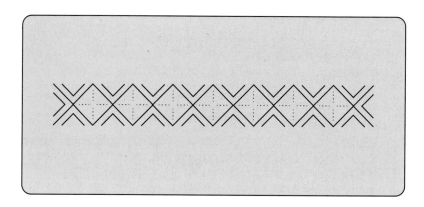

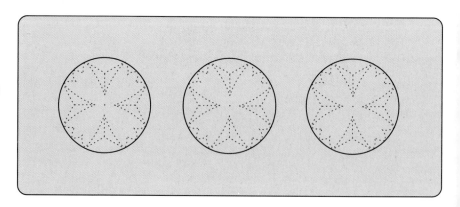

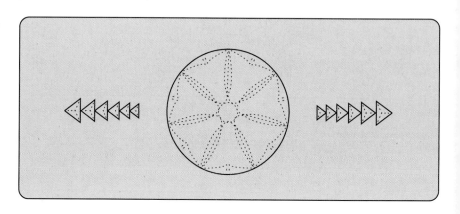

PROJECTS FOR CELEBRATING

Perpetual Calendar

By Marty Leenhouts

Kiss the old year goodbye (and usher in many new ones) with an elegant calendar that's useful and durable to boot. Use any or all of the patterns as desired; for instance, you could chip carve just the month and day blocks, leaving the box plain, or chip carve the box pieces and paint or woodburn the other elements. The font I selected for the months consists entirely of straight cuts, making it possible for you to find success carving letters that may have intimidated you in the past.

Preparing the Blanks

Pre-sand the blanks to 320-grit until no marks remain. Apply a gel stain to all of the pieces using a foam brush; I prefer gel stains because they dry on the surface and don't penetrate the wood like normal oil-based stains. This is ideal if you plan to carve through the stain for contrast between the carved and uncarved areas. After the stain has dried, apply the patterns using either a photocopy and a Pattern Transfer Tool or graphite transfer paper and a pencil. The pattern will be hard to see if a dark gel stain is used, so be sure to surround your carving setup with good, even lighting. Daylight-rated bulbs come in handy here.

Pattern Application

Carving numbers on the end grain of the blocks will be a challenge. Make it as easy as possible by applying numbers like 1 and 7 on the end grain because these numbers require just a few cuts to carve. Save numbers 8 and 5 for the face grain. Carving the correct numbers on each cube makes it possible to create all of the numbers needed for each day of the month. The number 6 will be flipped so you can also use it as a 9.

Carving and Finishing

Carve the pieces. To avoid chip-out in challenging areas, such as where several ray-shaped chips fan out along the top and sides of the box, practice this technique: make the first cut on each chip from the outside to the inside and carve from right to left. Maintain a light grip on your knife as you reach the delicate central area where all of the chips converge; a light grip results in a light cut. Make the second cut from the inside out, again keeping a light grip. Then continue switching back and forth until that row of chips is complete. This alternating approach will help preserve the intricate regions on the carving.

To remove any pattern lines, moisten a cotton cloth with lacquer thinner and gently wipe them off. Glue and clamp the box pieces together and let dry, making sure all edges sit squarely. Then spray the box and blocks with three to four coats of satin lacquer or clear matte acrylic and let dry. Fit all of the day and month blocks inside and display.

materials & **tools**

MATERIALS
- Basswood, ⅜" (1cm) thick: box sides, 2 each 2¾" x 4¼" (7cm x 10.8cm)
- Basswood, ⅜" (1cm) thick: box bottom, 2¾" x 6½" (7cm x 16.5cm)
- Basswood, ⅜" (1cm) thick: box top, 2¾" x 5½" (7cm x 14cm)
- Basswood, ⅜" (1cm) thick: box back, 6⅛" x 6½" (15.6cm x 16.5cm)
- Basswood, 1" (2.5cm) square: month blocks, 3 each 5½" (14cm) long
- Basswood, 2¾" (7cm) square: day blocks, 2 each 2¾" (7cm) long
- Sandpaper: assorted grits up to 320
- Graphite transfer paper
- Pencil
- Gel stain, such as Varathane® Ipswitch pine
- Wood glue or epoxy
- Clear finish, such as spray matte acrylic or satin lacquer
- Cotton cloth
- Lacquer thinner (optional)

TOOLS
- Chip carving knife, such as a diamond modified knife
- Pattern Transfer Tool (optional)
- Foam brush
- Clamps
- Square (optional)

The author used these products for the project. Substitute your choice of brands, tools, and materials as desired.

Perpetual Calendar
Cube 1 Patterns

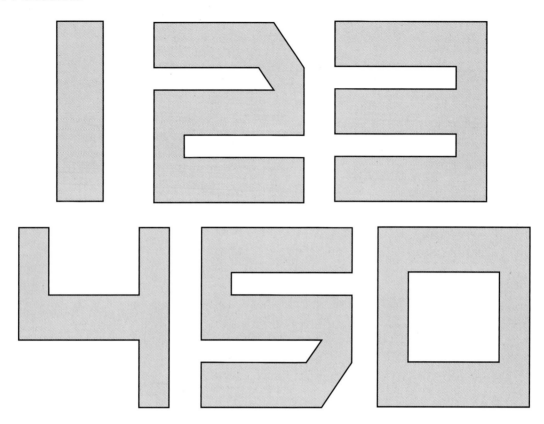

Perpetual Calendar
Cube 2 Patterns

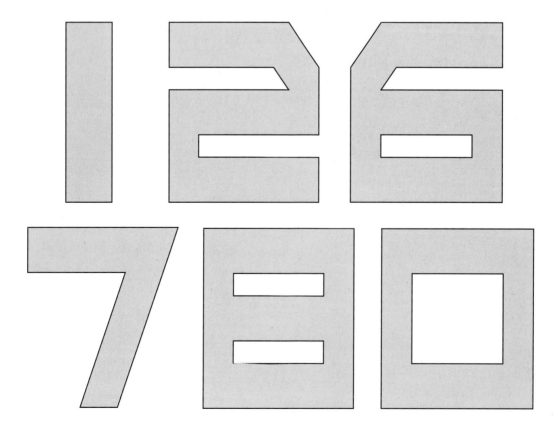

Perpetual Calendar Month Patterns

JANUARY

FEBRUARY

MARCH APRIL

MAY JUNE

JULY AUGUST

SEPTEMBER

OCTOBER

NOVEMBER

DECEMBER

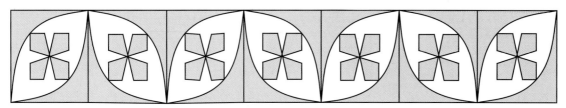

Top Flange

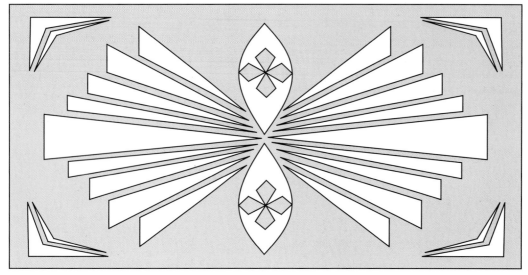

Box Top

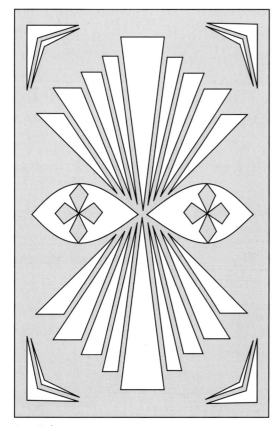

Box Sides

Perpetual Calendar Box Patterns

Bethlehem Star

By Marty Leenhouts

F or this design, I wanted to incorporate long, graceful lines that mimic a star's rays. You'll need to make several small, precise cuts to achieve that look, but the result is stunning. Use the star to top your tree or hang it elsewhere in the house—either way, it's an instant conversation piece.

materials & tools

MATERIALS

- Basswood, ⅜" (1cm) thick: 3½" x 8" (8.9cm x 20.3cm)
- Graphite transfer paper
- Pencil
- Sandpaper: 220-grit
- Tombow Sand Eraser (optional)
- Finish: satin spray lacquer or clear matte acrylic
- Gel stain (optional)
- Cotton cloth (optional)
- D-ring hanger (optional)
- Alligator clip (optional)
- Glue: cyanoacrylate (CA) (optional)

TOOLS

- Scroll saw or band saw
- Chip carving knife, such as a diamond modified knife
- Pattern Transfer Tool (optional)
- Vacuum
- Foam brush (optional)

The author used these products for the project. Substitute your choice of brands, tools, and materials as desired.

Prepping and Carving

Photocopy the pattern and use graphite paper to trace it onto the blank. Alternatively, secure a laser print or photocopy of the pattern facedown and use a heated tool, such as the Pattern Transfer Tool, to transfer the image to the wood. Cut the star on a band saw or scroll saw.

Carve the central flower and diamonds. Then add the decorative details around the flower. Many of the chips can be removed with two or three cuts. Keep the joint of your thumb on the thumb notch and try to visualize the point of your knife reaching the center of each chip. When the cuts meet, the chip will pop out. Remove all leftover pattern lines (I use a Tombow Sand Eraser). Be especially careful around the delicate side tips of the star, as they can easily break.

Finishing

You can finish the star in a number of ways. I chose a natural look. The easiest finish can be completed, beginning-to-end, in less than two hours. Spray two coats of satin lacquer or clear matte acrylic finish on the surface of the carving. Allow 30 minutes of dry time between coats. Lightly sand with 220-grit sandpaper, vacuum off the dust, and spray on a final coat.

If you do wish to add color to the star, carefully brush a gel stain into the recessed areas after your clear finish has dried. Wipe off any excess from the surface with a cotton cloth and let dry overnight. Apply more gel stain as needed; I add a final clear topcoat for a consistent finish.

Display as desired. If your star will be a wall piece, attach a D-ring hanger to the back. To make a unique tree topper, attach an alligator clip (available at craft stores) to the back of the star with cyanoacrylate (CA) glue. Clip the star to the top of your tree for all to see!

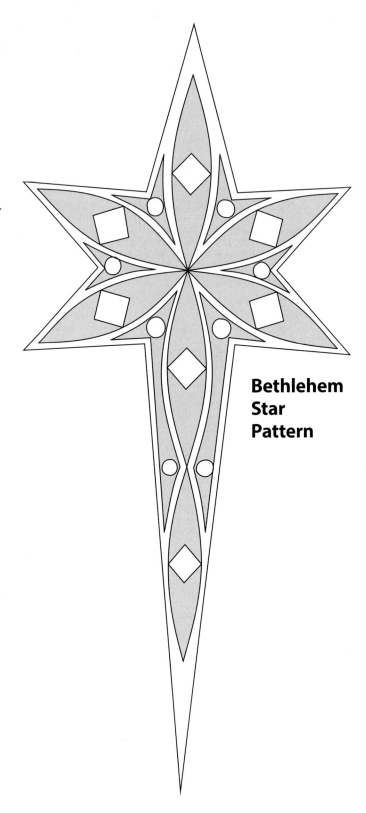

Bethlehem Star Pattern

Holiday Snowflakes

By Gary MacKay

These designs are easy to cut and carve. I cut the snowflakes on a scroll saw, but you could also carve the designs on round or square blanks. Mix and match the designs to create sets of unique ornaments.

Making the Ornaments

Attach the patterns to the basswood with spray adhesive. Drill a hole in each ornament with a ³⁄₃₂" (2.5mm)-dia. twist bit. Then cut the perimeter. You can carve directly through the paper, but for more accurate cuts, draw the patterns directly onto the wood. Soak the patterns with mineral spirits to remove them, and wipe off any excess adhesive with a rag soaked in mineral spirits. Sand carefully with 220-grit sandpaper to remove any fuzzies, making sure to not sand off the sharp corners of the chips. Apply a clear spray finish.

materials & **tools**

MATERIALS

- Basswood ¼" (6mm) thick: 5" (12.7cm) square (per ornament)
- Spray adhesive
- Mineral spirits
- Rag
- Sandpaper: 220-grit
- Finish: clear spray
- Colored ribbon or string

The author used these products for the project. Substitute your choice of brands, tools, and materials as desired.

TOOLS

- Scroll saw with blades: #5 reverse-tooth
- Drill with bit: ³⁄₃₂" (2.5mm)-dia. twist
- Chip carving knife

Troubleshooting Your Chips

A few things can go wrong when you chip carve. Here are a few examples of bad chips and how to prevent them.

Wavy edges like this appear for three reasons: a dull knife, starting and stopping repeatedly while cutting, or going back to try to clean up the cuts. Remember to strop often, position your hand so you can complete each cut in one smooth movement, and make sure any cuts you make to clean up the edges of the chip are at the same angle as the first cuts.

Fuzzy bits of wood left in the bottom of the chips appear when your cuts do not meet. Some larger chips require you to remove smaller chips first, but whenever possible, cut deep enough to free the chips the first time. If you do need to make multiple cuts, make sure you cut at the same angle. When in doubt, make your cut deeper to make sure you free the chip.

Sometimes you want a rounded corner, but in most cases, chip carving depends on uniform sharp corners. To carve sharp corners, make sure the cuts you use to free the chip meet exactly. If a chip doesn't pop out cleanly, chances are the corners will suffer.

³⁄₃₂"-diameter hole on all ornaments

Holiday Snowflake Patterns

**Holiday Snowflake
Patterns**

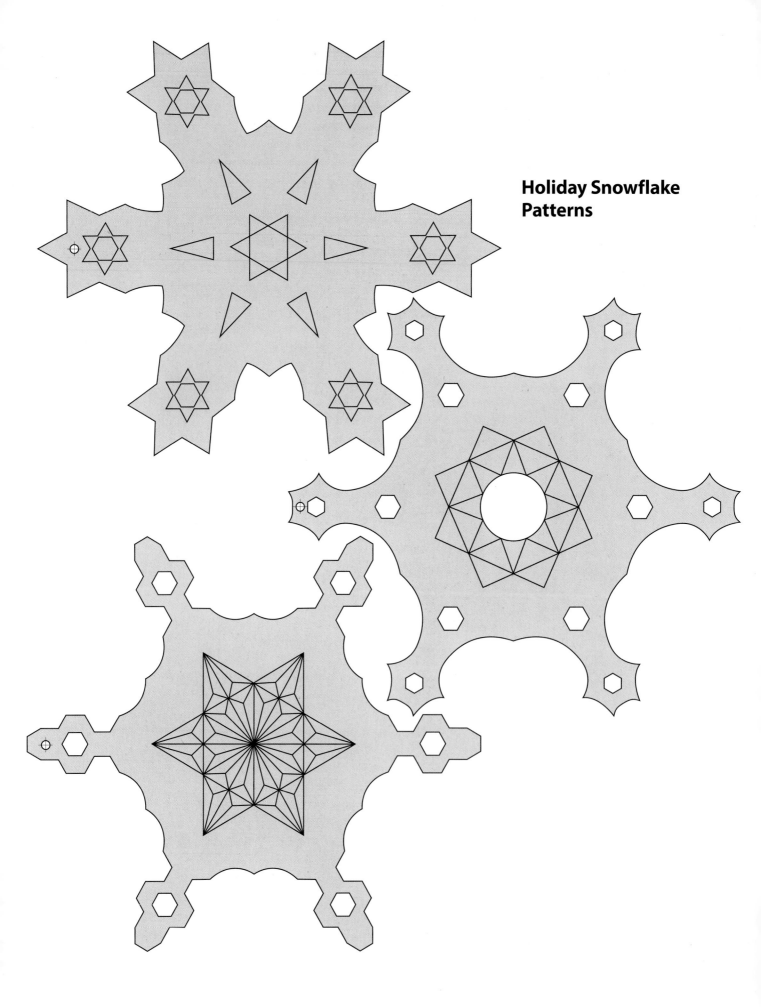

Holiday Snowflake Patterns

Holiday Snowflake Patterns

"Stained Glass" Baubles

By Bruce Nicholas

Let there be light! Add some additional sparkle to your holiday ornaments by piercing through the blank as you carve. This technique allows light to shine through the piece and gives ornaments a little something extra.

Preparing the Blanks

While it's possible to cut the pieces to their final shape after carving, it's easier to cut the blank to size first. I usually mass-produce blanks, and then transfer the pattern onto the project. To transfer the pattern, draw directly on the wood with a soft B-lead pencil. If you prefer to trace the pattern onto the wood, use Saral transfer paper, which can be removed with a regular eraser. Use caution on the precut blanks to make sure the pattern is aligned correctly. Drill a hole in each ornament with a ³⁄₃₂" (2.5mm)-dia. twist bit.

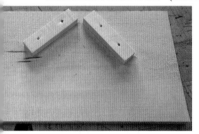

Carving Safely

Holding a small, thin blank safely can be a challenge. I created a jig to hold the blank as I carve, especially when I'm making the pierced cuts. Cut a piece of ⅜" (1cm)-thick plywood to 6" by 12" (15.2cm by 30.5cm), and cut two ½" by ½" by 3" (1.3cm by 1.3cm by 7.6cm) cleats. Screw or nail the cleats to the plywood at a 90° angle to each other, with a small gap at the point to allow the chips to escape. Hold the blank against the cleats as you carve to keep the sharp blade away from your body.

Making the Ornaments

Start with the largest chips first. When you carve the largest chips, the knife applies the greatest pressure on the walls around the chip. Do not try to remove these chips in one cut. Instead, make a series of cuts with the knife blade held at a consistent angle. Pay attention to the grain direction, because cross grain cuts tend to be the area where a chip hangs up when you try to remove it. Conversely, the blank can split when you are carving with the direction of the grain.

"Stained Glass" Baubles Pattern

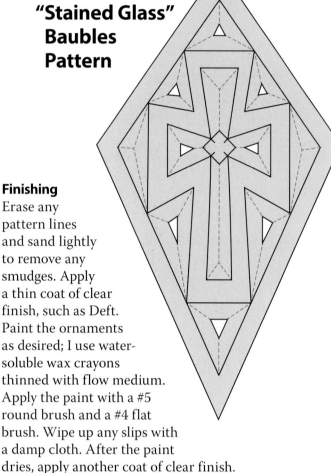

Finishing

Erase any pattern lines and sand lightly to remove any smudges. Apply a thin coat of clear finish, such as Deft. Paint the ornaments as desired; I use water-soluble wax crayons thinned with flow medium. Apply the paint with a #5 round brush and a #4 flat brush. Wipe up any slips with a damp cloth. After the paint dries, apply another coat of clear finish.

For a natural finish, add a few light coats of clear finish, but not enough so the finish looks glossy. Then apply a tinted wax. I mix clear finishing wax with a small amount of brown wax, and apply it with a medium stiff brush. Remove the excess wax with the same brush. The wax imparts just enough color to accent the carved design.

materials & tools

MATERIALS
- Basswood blanks, ¼" (6mm) thick: sized for patterns
- Saral transfer paper (optional)
- Pencil: B-lead, soft
- Eraser
- Sandpaper
- Clear spray finish, such as Deft®
- Wax crayons: water soluble
- Flow medium
- Finishing wax: clear, brown
- Cloth
- Colored ribbon or string

TOOLS
- Chip carving knife
- Shop-made jig (optional)
- Paintbrushes: #5 round, #4 flat, medium-sized stiff-bristle
- Drill with bit: ³⁄₃₂" (2.5mm)-dia. twist

The author used these products for the project. Substitute your choice of brands, tools, and materials as desired.

"Stained Glass" Baubles Patterns

Nostalgic Sleds

By Charlene Lynum

Having grown up in the Midwest, I have many fond memories of gliding downhill with my brothers, with the snow in our faces and our cheeks pink from the cold. Those days inspired these patterns. They use simple two- and three-corner chips that don't take days to master and look fantastic when they're complete.

materials & tools

MATERIALS

- Basswood, ¼" (6mm) thick: sled top, 1¾" x 3¼" (4.4cm x 8.3cm)
- Basswood, ¼" (6mm) thick: runners, 2 each ¾" x 4⅛" (1.9cm x 10.5cm)
- Scrap wood ¼" (6mm) thick: spacer, 1" x 2" (2.5cm x 5.1cm)
- Wood dowel, ⅛" (3mm)-dia.: 1½" (3.8cm) long
- Pencil (optional)
- Graphite transfer paper (optional)

- Tape: double-sided
- Wood glue
- Sandpaper: 220-grit
- Paper towels
- Finish, such as Minwax® clear satin fast-drying polyurethane
- Colored ribbon or string (optional)

TOOLS

- Scroll saw with blades: #5 reverse-tooth
- Drill with bit: ⅛" (3mm)-dia.
- Pattern Transfer Tool
- Chip carving knife
- Small weight

The author used these products for the project. Substitute your choice of brands, tools, and materials as desired.

Getting Started

Sand the blank with 220-grit sandpaper and attach the patterns; I ironed a laser copy on using a pattern transfer tool, but you can trace the designs on with graphite paper and a pencil, if desired. Be sure to place the pattern on the outward facing side of both runners. Orient the grain vertically along the length of the sled and runners. Cut the sled body with a scroll saw; I like to use a #5 reverse-tooth blade so I get a smooth cut on both the bottom and top of the project. (This reduces the amount of sanding needed.) I recommend stack-cutting the pieces for the runners so they're identical. Secure the stack with double-sided tape. Then drill the ⅛" (3mm)-dia. hole for the dowel while they're still stacked so the holes line up, and cut the runners.

Carving, Assembling, and Finishing

Carve the sled and runner designs. Always make sure to angle your blade so the deepest point coincides with the center of each chip. To assemble the sleds, slide the runners on the dowel with the carved sides out. Place a small amount of wood glue on each end of the dowel, and then slide a runner out to each end of the dowel, using the 1" (2.5cm) scrap spacer for correct spacing. Make sure the runners sit flat on the table. You may need to twist them on the dowel to make this happen, so adjust them before the glue dries.

Place the carved sled top on a solid surface with the carved side down. Place a very small ribbon of glue on the top edge of both runners. Center the runners on the bottom side of the sled top. Make sure the top of the runners (doweled end) and the top of the sled (the side that's curved outward) are on the same end. Remove any squeeze-out with a clean paper towel. Make sure that your spacer doesn't get glued to the sled, as you will discard it later. Place a small weight (e.g. can of soup) on the runners and allow to dry. Once the assembly has dried, remove the spacer. Apply a finish and display as desired; I used clear satin polyurethane and hung mine with colored ribbon.

Nostalgic Sled Patterns

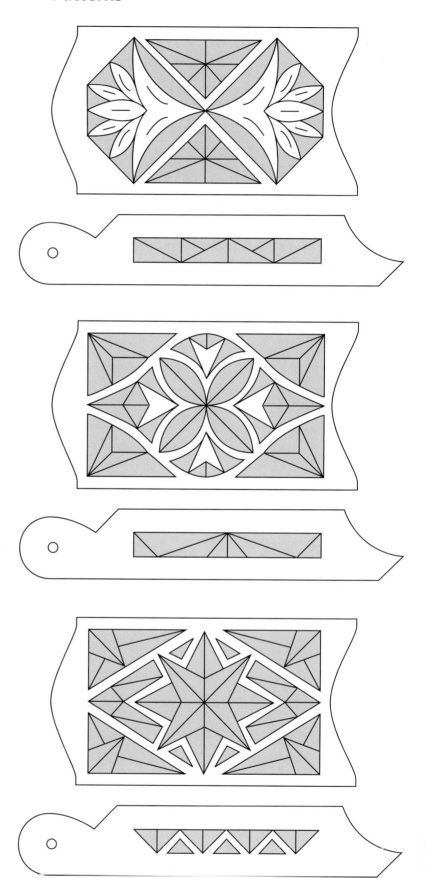

Classic Flower Ornament

By Wayne Barton

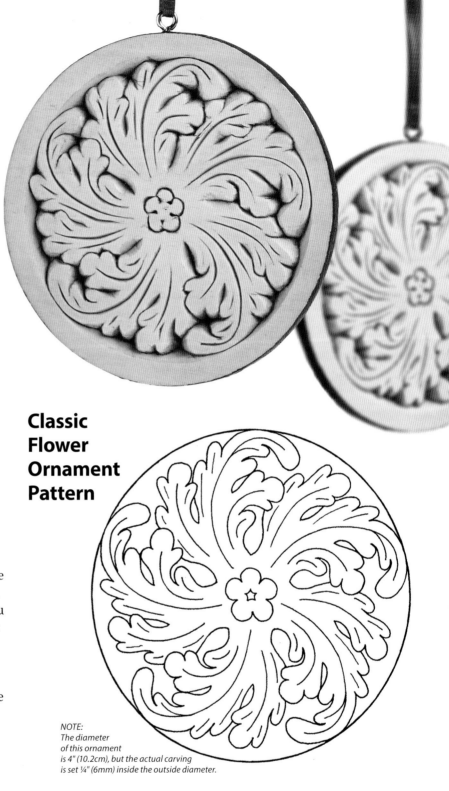

Chip carved ornaments are usually based on geometric figures. However, I decided to branch out and make an ornament with a more positive image and organic style. You can display the ornament alone, attach it to the top of a box, or even carve several to decorate a mantel or door frame.

Carving the Flower

Transfer the pattern to the wood with graphite paper. I always advise transferring the pattern with graphite paper so you can easily see if you are removing or cracking away wood that isn't supposed to be removed.

As you carve the flower, hold the blade at approximately a 65° angle to the wood. When making tight or small curved cuts, raise the angled blade up so it's more on its tip, reducing the amount of metal in the wood. Don't cut deeper than necessary to remove the chips. Keep the "vein" lines narrow so they don't overpower the carving. If desired, add a scalloped border on the back side of the ornament.

Finishing the Flower

Spray both sides of the ornament with three coats of polyurethane, such as Minwax®. If desired, paint the outer edge and add a message on the back. Apply a light brown finishing wax, such as Briwax®, to both sides of the ornament to emphasize the carved areas while preserving a natural appearance.

Classic Flower Ornament Pattern

NOTE:
The diameter of this ornament is 4" (10.2cm), but the actual carving is set ¼" (6mm) inside the outside diameter.

materials & **tools**

MATERIALS	TOOLS
• Basswood, ⅜" (1cm) thick: 5" (12.7cm) square	• Chip carving knife
• Graphite transfer paper	• Foam brush (for applying wax)
• Pencil	• Paintbrush (optional)
• Spray polyurethane, such as Minwax®	
• Paint (optional)	*The author used these products for the project. Substitute your choice of brands, tools, and materials as desired.*
• Colored wax, such as Briwax®: light brown	

About the Contributors

This book would not have been possible without our talented contributors. We hope you enjoy learning more about their creative journeys. Be sure to visit their websites and reach out to them on social media as you embark on your own creative pursuits.

Amy Costello is known for her delicate chip carving on turnings and small joinery projects. While she has built furniture in several industrial-sized shops since starting in 2014, she currently does all of her woodworking on a 6' by 10' platform in her bedroom, with a long curtain splitting the room. When she's not in the shop, Amy enjoys illustrating, throwing pots, and playing Dungeons and Dragons. Find her on Instagram @amy.makes. everything or amymakeseverything.com.

Barry McKenzie is a popular instructor and owner of the School of Chip Carving. He has several instructional and pattern booklets available. Barry also writes a regular chip carving newsletter.

Ben Mayfield of Orem, Utah, has been carving for several years. He also prospects for gold. His work has been displayed at a local woodcarving supply store and at the Springville (Utah) Museum of Art. You can reach Ben at benkmayfield@yahoo.com.

Bruce Nicholas discovered chip carving during the 1980s. He has taken several classes and made four trips to Switzerland to research chip carving at its source. He teaches the art at his studio near St. Paris, Ohio, and across the Midwest. Bruce also retails a line of tools, projects, and patterns related to chip carving.

Charlene Lynum began chip carving around 1985. She lives near Eau Claire, Wis., and is a member of the West Wisconsin Woodcarvers Guild. What started out as a hobby has turned into an artistic adventure over the past few years. She appreciates the simple beauty that chip carving can add to a project. Find her on Instagram @thelynums.

Deanna Cadoret lives in Canada with a large family of animals. Besides chip carving, she loves working with yarn, drawing, and painting. Deanna has previously published a tutorial called "Stone Wall—Watercolour over Pen and Ink" on Wetcanvas.com under the screen name Kitaye.

Steve Reed started carving more than 30 years ago while serving in the U.S. Air Force. An award-winning carver and competition judge, he currently teaches chip and figure carving for Midwest Woodworkers Inc. in Omaha, Neb. A member of the National Woodcarvers Association and Mid-America Woodcarvers Association, Steve lives in Bellevue, Neb. with his wife, Cathy.

Gary MacKay of Myrtle Beach, S.C., is the author of *Box-Making Projects for the Scroll Saw*, available from Fox Chapel Publishing, foxchapelpublishing.com.

Tatiana Baldina is a professional woodcarving artist with a degree in Applied Fine Arts from the Volga Regional State University, and lives and works in Zhigulevsk, Russia. Tatiana specializes in chip carving on basswood and has been a freelance woodcarver since 2014. Find her on Instagram @tatbalcarvings.

Marty Leenhouts is a regular contributor to *Woodcarving Illustrated* and the author of *Chip Carving Essentials: A Step-By-Step Guide to Successful Chip Carving*. The owner of MyChipCarving.com and EZcarving.com, he has 30 years of teaching experience. His instructional videos have 3+ million views and can be found on YouTube under MyChipCarving.

Tom Noller started carving in 2009 after retiring as an engineer. He is the president and newsletter editor for the Lake Ray Hubbard Woodcarving Club, located in Rowlett, Texas.

Roman Chernikov is a software engineer who has been carving as a hobby since 2013. He lives near San Francisco and attends the Santa Clara Valley Carvers Club. For more of his work or to purchase the practice board mentioned in this article, visit readNtry.com.

Vernon DePauw started carving in seventh-grade shop class and has been carving for pleasure and profit ever since. For more of his work, visit his website at vldwoodcarver.com.

Roman and Olga Repikova have been carving for 12 years. Great lovers of music, they manufacture ukuleles and other handmade wooden items at their home in Ukraine. Contact them at woodcrafttt@gmail.com or on Etsy at WoodCarv.

Wayne Barton is credited with creating the renaissance of chip carving to the United States. He was named Woodcarver of the Year by *Woodcarving Illustrated* in 2005. Wayne has written several books, and he teaches seminars around the country. He frequently leads tours of Switzerland, where he learned to chip carve. For more information, visit his website at chipcarving.com.

Index

Note: Page numbers in italics indicate projects.